Western Memorabilia and Collectibles

ROBERT W.D. BALL

Price Guide Included

77 Lower Valley Road, Atglen, PA 19310

Above:

Worn by equestrian star, Lynn Randall, these western dress elements reflect the lavish rodeo parade look, circa 1960. The custom, rhinestone-trimmed hat is by Donhoy. The red satin shirt, tailored by Maude McMorries, incorporates scalloped yoke and cuffs, rhinestone accents and pearl snap fasteners. The Justin boot is finished in rare, South American Geoffroy's cat.

National Cowboy Hall of Fame and Western Heritage Center

Back cover:

These Buffalo Bill effects, include a Fred Ross saddle with Cody's Mexican spurs, a Winchester Deluxe Model 1886 rifle, a tour book of Great Britain, a photo of Cody on a galloping horse, a copy of the *Buffalo Bill Weekly*, a Presentation Model 1860 U.S. Staff and Field Officer's sword presented by Cody, an elk hide frontiersman's jacket used in his show, all surrounding a framed poster of "Buffalo Bill, Chief of Scouts and Guide for the U.S.Army."

Witherell's Americana Auctions

Front cover:

Dating from the 1890s to the 1960s, this grouping includes an early, scalloped-top western boot that carries an Oscar Crockett spur with R.T. Frazier strap, a braided rawhide riata fashioned by Luis Ortega, spotted "woolie" chaps by C.P. Shipley, and a well-worn Stetson made famous by actor Walter Brennan.

National Cowboy Hall of Fame and Western Heritage Center

Published by Schiffer Publishing, Ltd.
77 Lower Valley Road
Atglen, PA 19310
Please write for a free catalog.
This book may be purchased from the publisher.
Please include $2.95 postage.
Try your bookstore first.

We are interested in hearing from authors
with book ideas on related subjects.

Printed in the United States of America.
ISBN: 0-88740-484-7

Acknowledgements

Witherell's Americana Auctions
P.O.Box 804
Healdsburg, CA 95448
(707)433-8950

Cheryl Steenerson and Chris Wolfe
Arizona State Parks
Phoenix, AZ

Richard A. Bourne Co., Inc.
Corporation Rd.
Hyannis, MA 02601

Dennis Bailey
49 Lysia St.
Fulham, London
SW6 6NF
England

The Jordan Gallery
1349 Sheridan Ave.
Cody, WY 82414

Jerry and Ruth Murphey
10701 Timbergrove La.
Corpus Christi, TX 78410

"Mac" Meckensturm
Portland, Conn.

Jack and Virginia Wigglesworth
Chevy Chase, MD

Don Sweet
Billy the Kid Museum
1601 E. Sumner
Fort Sumner, NM 88119
(505) 355-2380

Richard Rattenbury, Curator
National Cowboy Hall of Fame
1700 N.E.63rd St.
Oklahoma City, OK 73111
(405)478-2250

Floretta Carter
Pioneer Museum
430 W 4th St.
Ashland, KS 67831

Table of Contents

Foreword

Due to an unrelenting work load and other pressing obligations, Ed Vebell was unable to participate in this sequel to "Cowboy Collectibles and Western Memorabilia." Ed's special insight and skills will be sorely missed, but I look forward to collaborating with him on future endeavors.

Since publication of "Cowboy Collectibles and Western Memorabilia," it has been gratifying to receive many requests from readers and collectors asking that a sequel be considered that would explore other collectibles as well as expand on the subjects previously covered. This volume is the result, and I trust it will add yet another dimension to the continuing saga of the Old West.

Introduction

With the slow, steady expansion of the West came those many influences for good and evil that have affected humanity over the centuries: Indians were slaughtered in the name of progress, the profit motive became all important to the early land barons, railroads fought for rights-of-way across virgin territory, and prisons were built to house the law breakers who rode the tides of expansion. The development of the west also brought the frontier doctors and teachers, who, under the most primitive conditions, eventually treated and taught—Indians and the new settlers. Rudimentary law came to the frontier in the form of local lawmen, U.S. Marshals, and traveling circuit court judges, who freely dispensed justice...sometimes from the muzzle of a Colt .44, or at the end of a hangman's rope, as witness Judge Roy Bean!

Sod huts were replaced with simple frame dwellings, which in turn evolved into substantial homesteads. As the neverending challenges of the frontier became less harsh, traces of gentility emerged. Frontier towns lost their false-front look and became permanent settling places. The distance between town, farm and ranch grew smaller with the advent of each new settlement. Migration became easier, with less perils than plaqued the earlier westward movement. Railroads eventually connected these tiny hamlets, many of which evolved into towns and cities reminiscent of their counterparts to the East and the telegraph provided immediate communication. A variety of products and goods could now move freely in all directions. Even the latest fashion designs from the East and Europe, became available to the dressmakers of the wealthy and fashion conscious women of the West.

Nevertheless, life was rarely easy on the frontier. Well into the present century, conditions remained harsh for all but the most fortunate, and as the frontiers of the West continued to expand, most ranch owners and individual settlers had to be enormously self-sufficient to cope.

In my previous book, "Cowboy Collectibles and Western Memorabilia," the emphasis was on the clothing worn, the equipment carried and used, and the ways people sought relaxation. In addition to items not previously shown, this book will focus on many similar aspects of the Western culture that were also an integral part of the history of the American West. Here you will see such diverse operations as the Territorial Prison at Yuma, Arizona in the late 1800s, the tools used in a frontier blacksmith shop, the interior of an early western barber shop and the printing presses and "Inter type" machine that printed the first weekly newspaper in Ashland, Kansas. For aficionados and novices alike, all these, and more, will hopefully, add another dimension to the subject, while, at the same time, elaborating on the mystique that gives the Old West its very special place in the hearts of so many.

Magnificent Double Caille "Centaur" Upright 25-cent and 50-cent Slot Machine. Lavishly embellished nickel trim on an oak cabinet in the Victorian style, the action starts when a coin is dropped in one or all six slots, with each slot's color corresponding to the like color on the wheel. Pushing down on the lever on the coin head registers the bet, and pushing the front handles releases the notched wheel, allowing it to spin. Circa 1900.

Witherell's Americana Auctions

Life on the Frontier

As settlements sprang up on the prairies, civilizing influences gradually took root. Stores with false fronts gave way to more permanent structures. Churches were erected, businesses were opened, and simple schoolhouses were built. Newspapers provided rudimentary news and towns eventually adopted self-government, with all the resultant problems and satisfactions. Eventually, stability began to be felt throughout the frontier.

However, these first settlements of the frontier brought with them the seeds of the social problems of the time. Many of the fledgling businesses were saloons and gambling establishments, the ever present "fancy women" following not far behind. Arguments were settled with drawn Colts and Smith and Wessons, and lawlessness frequently ran unchecked.

From the humble to the exotic, on the following pages you will find many examples of those items our forefathers used on a daily basis. Here also are relics of heroes of the day, as well as the anti-hero—in this case, Billy the Kid.

Barbershop from Ashland, Kansas as it appeared at the turn of the century. Please note the original barber pole, hair ointments, shaving mugs and signs. Of special interest is the tin bathtub. The cowboys took a bath there once a week for 25 cents, or those on cattle drives may have come in and bathed. In the foreground is an old foot-driven Singer sewing machine for on-the-spot repairs. The ladies, with the advent of electricity, could indulge in a permanent wave with the octopus-like machine next to the tub.

Pioneer Museum, Ashland, Kansas

FRONTIER DOCTOR

Thomas H. Wigglesworth was known as the "Pathfinder of the San Juan," because of his ability as a location engineer for the D. & R. G. of Colorado. He made many railroad surveys, including the route between Silverton and Durango. In the late 1880s, he and his wife, with their five children located on their famous Waterfall Ranch in the Animas Valley. One of their sons, Albert, was crippled in one leg from an infantile disease, probably polio, of which nothing was known at that time. Because of this handicap he could not make a living as a ranch-hand, so his parents decided to educate him as a doctor.

Attending the State University at Boulder, Albert, or Al as he was called, graduated in 1896. The field of medicine was extremely crowded and a hospital internship very difficult to obtain, so Al interned with various doctors. He wandered around the southwest, including Mexico, gaining knowledge and experience. Having taken a civil service exam at one point in his training days, he was offered the position of doctor at the Fort Lewis Indian School near Durango in November, 1900. It was there that he met his future wife, Miss Edna

Wright of Washington, D.C., the kindergarten teacher.

Albert Wigglesworth remained in the Indian Service until 1925, at which point he transferred to the Veteran's Bureau, as it was then known. During the time he was in the Indian Service, he also served as Medical Officer at Albuquerque from 1918 to 1924, when he was put in charge of all the medical services to all Pueblos in the Rio Grande Basin of New Mexico.

Working under the most primitive of conditions, Dr. Albert Wigglesworth devoted a great part of his life to alleviating the suffering among the many tribal members of the area. For this, he will always be remembered and his memory will live on.

Doctor's office, circa 1895, with the addition of electrical apparatus added as it became available. This office reflects the equipment that was used during these early days, with the enameled wash basins, pitchers, etc. the forerunners of piped in city water. Note the sterilizer and scales on the shelves at the rear.

Pioneer Museum, Ashland, Kansas

A ranch house kitchen from the turn of the century, before the advent of rural electrification. To the right are the oil lamps that provided the illumination at meal times, while on the floor are the butter churn and coal scuttle familiar to every household of those days. Notice the cooking implements on the stove which were large enough to provide the necessary hardy meals required by hard working men. Items such as these may still be found by collectors.

Pioneer Museum, Ashland, Kansas

An early map of Clark County, Kansas, showing the old Indian trails and cattle trails that crossed the county. Note the indication of the last time a herd of buffalo was spotted in 1874.

Pioneer Museum, Ashland, Kansas

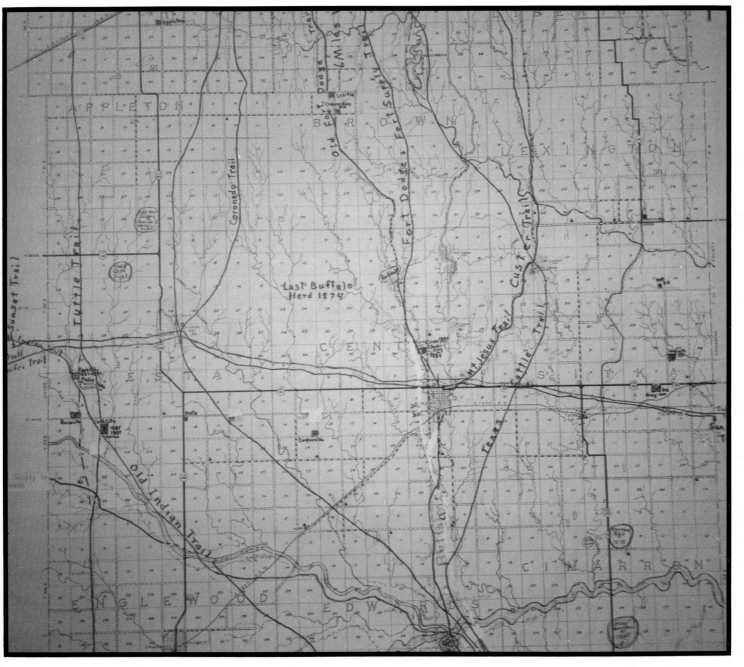

The printing presses and "Intertype" machine used in the first weekly newspaper office in Ashland, Kansas.

Pioneer Museum, Ashland, Kansas

Opposite page top:

Lovely carved furniture from the homestead of Mr. and Mrs. J.B. Smith, who lived northwest of the Clark County State Lake, Kansas in 1885. The black dress is a wedding dress worn at that time by a Mrs. Ainsworth, while the hat is contemporary to the dress. Note the period doll to the left of the mannikin.

Pioneer Museum, Ashland, Kansas

Opposite page bottom:

Pump organ made by Cornish and Co., Washington, New Jersey. James Oscar Johnston bought this for $50 for his wife, Mary Ellen, in 1882, the first Christmas they were married. His brothers and sisters picked wild berries in Missouri to help pay for the organ.

Pioneer Museum, Ashland, Kansas

A display of different styles of bits.

Pioneer Museum, Ashland, Kansas

Opposite page top:

The interior of a blacksmith shop from Englewood, Kansas. On the back wall are displayed the various tools used, while an early drill press is seen to the right, with a grinding wheel to its right. Note the quenching tub on the floor to the left of the picture. Tools such as these may be found today by the ardent collector, while horse shoes in different styles and sizes add to a collection.

Pioneer Museum, Ashland, Kansas

Opposite page bottom:

An authentic chuck wagon from the last century, illustrating the various iron pots used in the foreground, both covered and uncovered. On the wagon itself may be seen large covered containers and baking pans. Notice the very large coffee pot half-hidden by the framed information. To the left of the chuck wagon may be seen a number of different branding irons.

Pioneer Museum, Ashland, Kansas

Chassis of the first hand-drawn fire wagon used in Minneola, Kansas. A glass container filled with sulfuric acid was placed under the black dome. When pressure was needed, the glass container was broken by raising the handle, thus breaking the glass and pressurizing the tank in order to put out the fire.

Pioneer Museum, Ashland, Kansas

Turn-of-the-century horse drawn fringed-top surrey, usually reserved for special occasions, such as weddings and outings.

Pioneer Museum, Ashland, Kansas

Early buggies used in the West. Note that the buggy on the right is a mail buggy used at Colonias, New Mexico from 1890 right into the early 1900s. To the left of the mail buggy is a two-seated buggy, then a three-seated buggy, followed by a frontier hearse.

Billy the Kid Museum

A close-up shot of the hearse, showing the reeded pilasters and ornate somber decorations, totally in fitting with the occasion.

Billy the Kid Museum

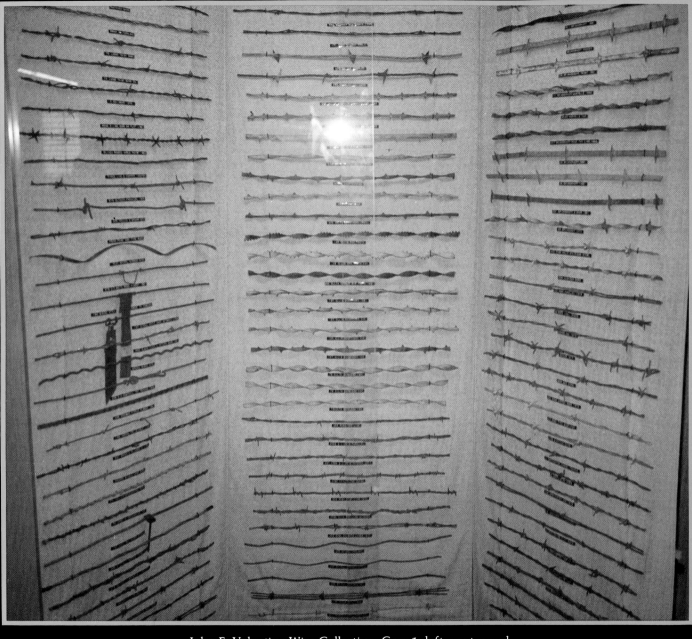

John F. Valentine Wire Collection, Case 1, left, center and
right panels.

Pioneer Museum, Ashland, Kansas

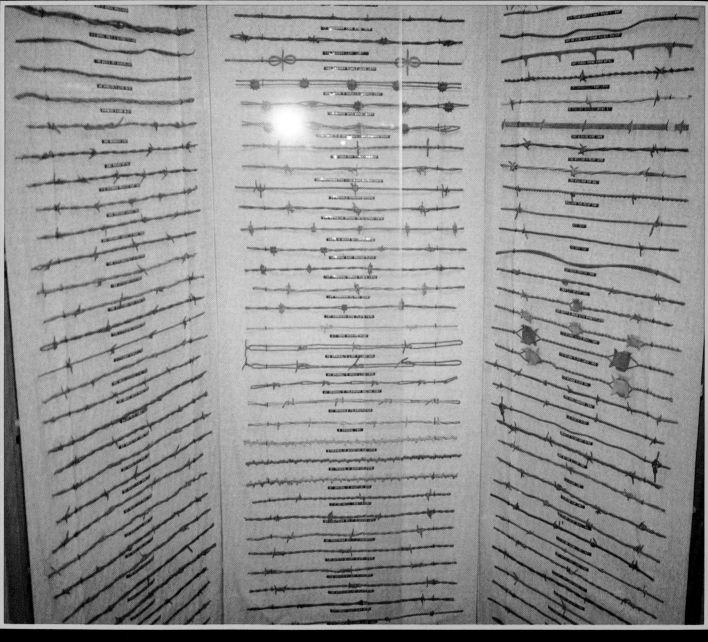

John F. Valentine Wire Collection, Case 2, left, center and
right panels.

Pioneer Museum, Ashland, Kansas

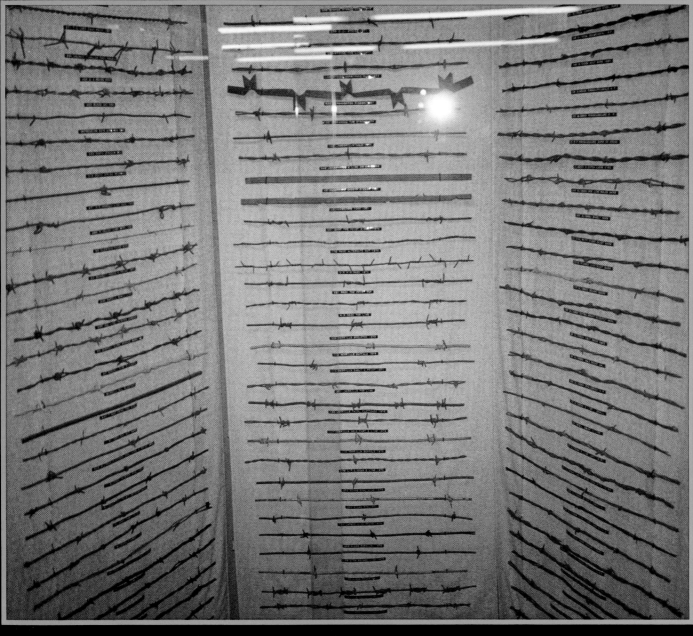

John F. Valentine Wire Collection, Case 3, left, center and right panels.

Pioneer Museum, Ashland, Kansas

John F. Valentine Wire Collection, Case 4, left, center and
right panels.

Pioneer Museum, Ashland, Kansas

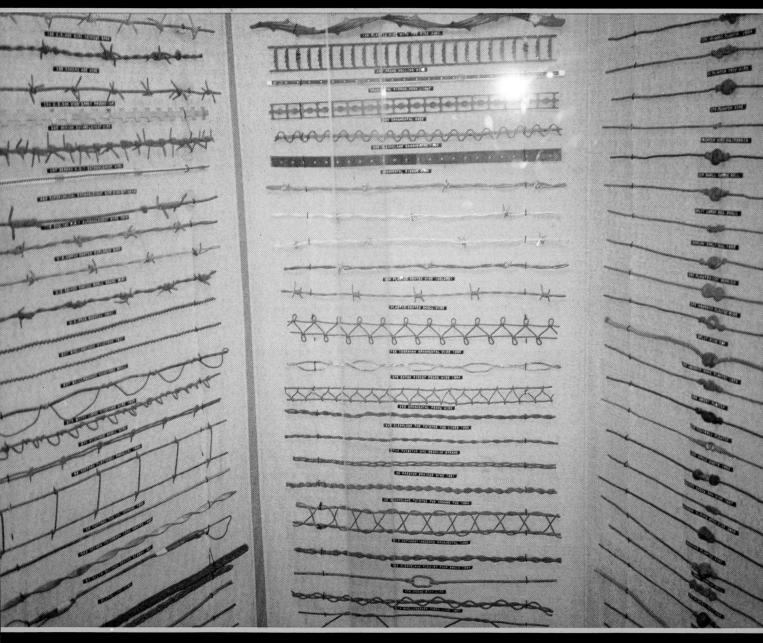

John F. Valentine Wire Collection, Case 5, left, center and right panels.

Pioneer Museum, Ashland, Kansas

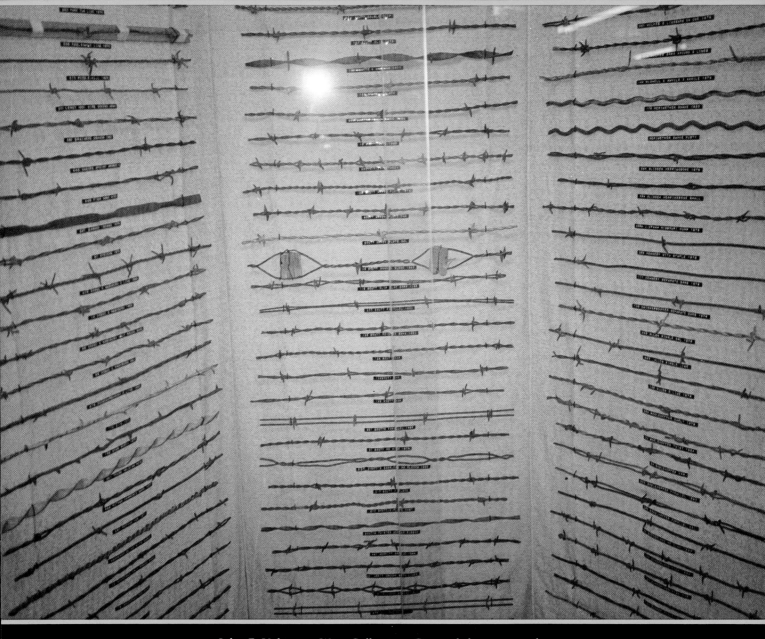

John F. Valentine Wire Collection, Case 6, left, center and
right panels.

Pioneer Museum, Ashland, Kansas

Early unmarked working saddle in well cared for condition. Note the high cantle and fork.

Billy the Kid Museum

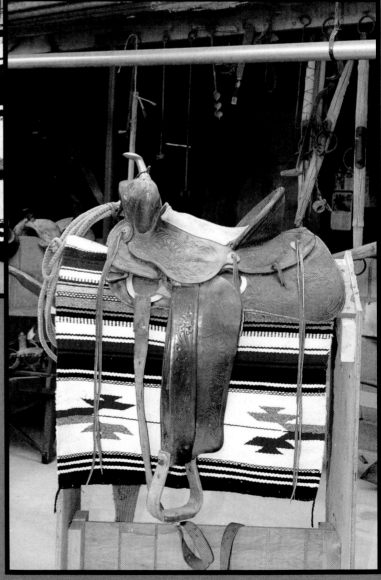

Nicely tooled Frazier saddle with high cantle and horn, used by Tom Duncan from 1928 to 1975.

Billy the Kid Museum

Lovely Hereford Brand saddle made by the Texas Tanning Manufacturing Co. of Yockum, Texas. This saddle was owned by Walter Wright of Fort Sumner, New Mexico, who purchased it from the Carr Lumber Co., circa 1922.

Billy the Kid Museum

Saddle made by Herb Wilmeth, Clovis, New Mexico, circa 1950.

Billy the Kid Museum

Saddle for a child as made for Sears and Roebuck.

Billy the Kid Museum

Saddle made by S.D. Myer, El Paso, Texas. This saddle was purchased by Dee Inman in Silver City, New Mexico in 1935 and was used in the Black Range Mountains.

Billy the Kid Museum

Mexican saddle, very similar to the 1850's Hope, or "Spanish" saddle, with its heavy wood fork and horn.

Billy the Kid Museum

Early form of pack saddle.

Billy the Kid Museum

Early pack saddle used to haul water kegs.

Billy the Kid Museum

25

Military pack saddle used for the transportation of ammunition.

Billy the Kid Museum

Saddle by "N. Porter, Abilene, Texas," No. 78. Note the round wooden stirrups and the original braided leather lariat. This is believed to be one of the earliest Porter saddles made, about 1885.

Dennis Bailey

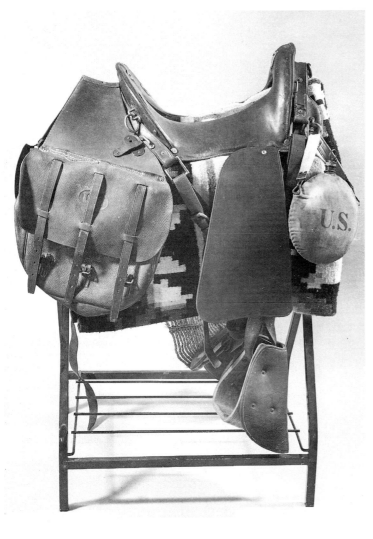

Military leather saddle, the cantle with brass shield marked "11 inch seat," the 1880s period canteen and the brown "US" leather saddle bags, all on an Indian blanket.

Richard A. Bourne Co., Inc.

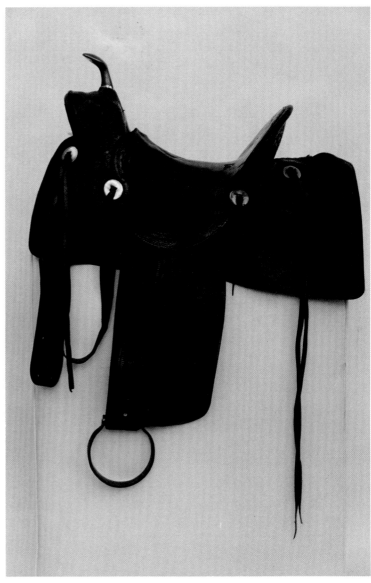

Buffalo Bill Cody's leather saddle, made by Fred Ross, Craig, Colorado and so stamped in three places. Carved with rosettes, elk, wild horses and kissing doves. Used by Buffalo Bill at the T.E. Ranch.

Witherell's Americana Auctions

Heavily studded leather parade saddle, measuring 50" by 29". This is of more recent vintage.

Witherell's Americana Auctions

Sterling silver Bolin parade saddle, manufactured by Edward H. Bolin Saddlers and Silversmiths, Hollywood, California. Black tooled leather, applied sterling, tie conchos, plus round and diamond sterling ornamentation. The applied sterling vignettes depict bulldogging, calf roping, bull riding, bronco busting and steer heads. This is repeated on both sides, along with a buffalo head adorning the saddle horn. This saddle, according to the present owner, appeared in 17 Rose Bowl Parades.

Witherell's Americana Auctions

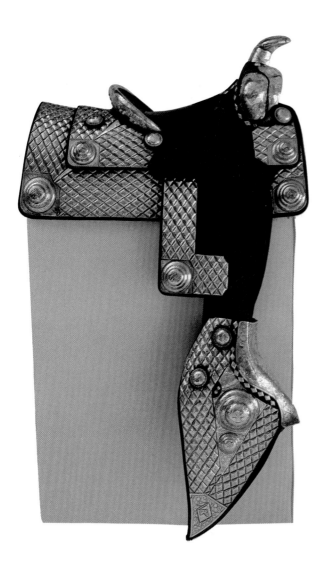

Gold and sterling silver mounted parade saddle. A triumph in art and craftsmanship, this is one of the most highly embellished silver saddles extant. It is a beautiful brown, highly tooled leather saddle with approximately fifteen hundred individual hand-engraved sterling silver attachments and fourteen attached gold horse heads. Silver marked, Don Ellis Co., Seattle, Washington. Complete with silver mounted breast plate. Circa 1940.

Witherell's Americana Auctions

Front view of the gold and sterling silver mounted parade saddle.

Witherell's Americana Auctions

Important Elk Hide Frontiersman Jacket, as used in the Wild West Show, most probably by Buffalo Bill himself. The jacket is decorated with elk tooth buttons, beading and fringe. Provenance: Julia Cody Goodman

Witherell's Americana Auctions

Well worn buckskin jacket, apparently custom made.

Dennis Bailey

Buckskin waistcoat, reputedly Apache, with cowrie shell decorations. Interestingly enough, there is a bullet hole through the back of the jacket with old blood stains.

Dennis Bailey

Black angora chaps belonging to Billy the Kid. Note the silver wrapped spurs at the bottom of the chaps. These were also the property of the Kid.

Billy the Kid Museum

An early pair of fringed shotgun chaps with pockets.

Billy the Kid Museum

Very unusually decorated open-back chaps. Please note the copper studding and the art work below each pocket. The belt is also able to substitute for a bronco-busting belt, being 8" wide. The right leg also sports a thong for a holster tie-down.

Dennis Bailey

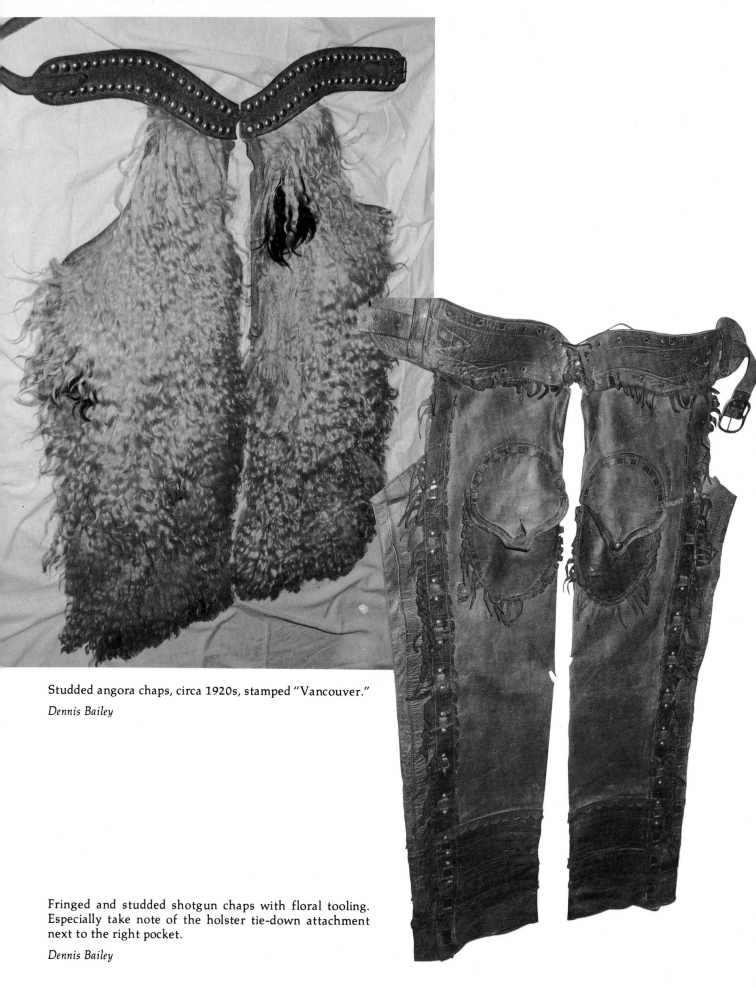

Studded angora chaps, circa 1920s, stamped "Vancouver."

Dennis Bailey

Fringed and studded shotgun chaps with floral tooling. Especially take note of the holster tie-down attachment next to the right pocket.

Dennis Bailey

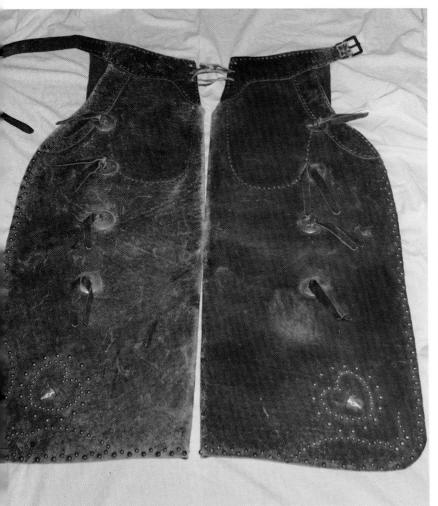

Heavily studded cuffs, with the buckles engraved with th[e] letter "M."

Dennis Bailey

Batwing chaps, with the belt stamped "N. Porter, Phoenix, Arizona," circa 1900. Note the conchos with rawhide ties, the fine stud work around the pockets, as well as the heart-shaped motif with silver steer head.

Dennis Bailey

Early spurs, stamped "J.W.Gibbon/Sweetwater, Texas."

Dennis Bailey

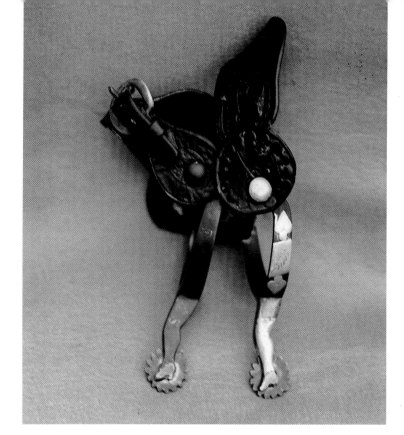

Gal leg spurs marked with the initials "E.S.," with tooled leather straps showing "Made on 101 Ranch Bliss Okla." within a circle. Note the heart motif in silver.

Jerry and Ruth Murphey

Pair of fringed leather gauntlets, with beaded decorations in a floral pattern. Nez Perce, circa 1920.

Witherell's Americana Auctions

Buffalo Bill Cody's spurs. These Mexican spurs of Col. W.F. Cody were given to Lyle Ellis by Mrs. H.T. Newell who operated the Irma Hotel, Cody, Wyoming, together with a photograph of Cody on a galloping horse, signed "W.F. Cody, Buffalo Bill 1907, to Julia."

Witherell's Americana Auctions

Engraved spurs with Mexican-style rowels and jangles, circa 1900. Note the elaborate tooling on the leathers.

Dennis Bailey

Cowboy pocket knife with 11 blades and tools, made by the Stiletto Cutlery Co. The ivory handles have "Ponca City" engraved on a silver shield on one side, while "101" is carved on the opposite handle. These are said to have been a Christmas gift one year for the 101 Ranch employees.

Jerry and Ruth Murphey

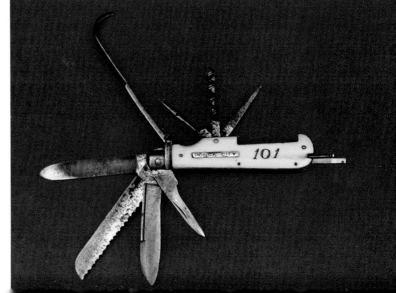

Proprietary circle mark used on all items made in the leather shop on the 101 Ranch.

Jerry and Ruth Murphey

Rare early watch fob, showing the heads of the three Miller Brothers of the 101 Ranch. Originally silver-plated, most of the plating has worn off with time, showing the bronze casting. These were made by Guinti Manufacturing Co., Providence, Rhode Island.

Jerry and Ruth Murphey

Photo of 101 Ranch cowboy, who seems rather proud of his "101" boots. Circa 1920s.

Jerry and Ruth Murphey

Close-up of the watch fob.

Jerry and Ruth Murphey

Leather notebook cover for holding a note pad used to record purchases and sales of cattle. The owner's initials are embossed on the front, while the back is marked "Made on 101 Ranch, Bliss, Okla." in a circle. This is the mark used on all items made in the 101 Ranch leather shop on the 101 Ranch.

Jerry and Ruth Murphey

Cast aluminum boot jack given to Herndon Davis with the boots. These jacks were cast in Arkansas, Kansas, just across the Oklahoma border.

Jerry and Ruth Murphey

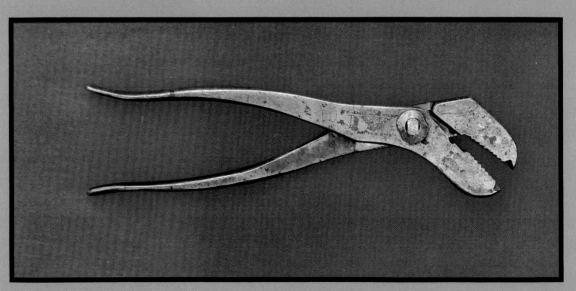

Fence pliers used on the 101 Ranch (note the "101" on the shank.). These belonged to J.O. Weldon, Head Foreman of the Agriculture department of the 101 Ranch for 22 years.

Jerry and Ruth Murphey

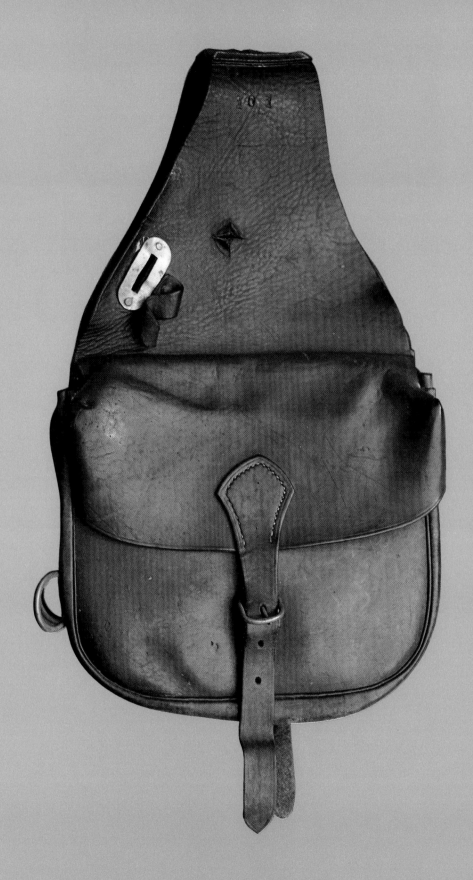

Military surplus cavalry saddle bags, purchased and die stamped by the 101 Ranch. This was the normal procedure with all items belonging to the Ranch.

Jerry and Ruth Murphey

Zack Miller had these elk hide boots made and gave them to Herndon Davis, in appreciation of a series of paintings that he did on the 101 Ranch in the 1920s.

Jerry and Ruth Murphey

Cowboy's leather wrist cuff, proudly marked 101 by the owner. 101 Cowboys marked "101" on all of their personal items.

Jerry and Ruth Murphey

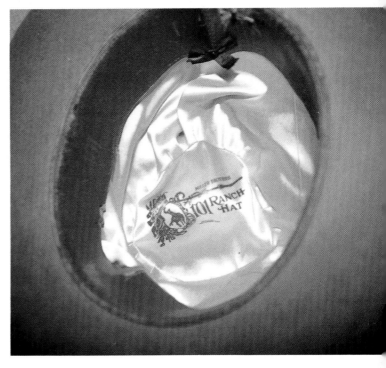

Miller Brothers 101 Ranch hat made for the ranch. These hats were sold in the store on the ranch.

Jerry and Ruth Murphey

Interior of the 101 Ranch hat. Note the white satin lining with the 101 Ranch logo in red. The band is marked "Six X Quality."

Jerry and Ruth Murphy

101 Ranch poster, copyright 1914 by the Strobridge Litho Co., Cincinnati and New York. Measures 20" by 30".

Jerry and Ruth Murphey

Two well-worn classic western style hats. The black hat belonged to Tex Shirley, while the white one belonged to Tom Duncan, both residents of De Baca County, New Mexico and a pair of early cowboys.

Billy the Kid Museum

Folding Faro layout, manufactured by George Masion &
Co., Denver, Colorado. Layouts were used to organize the
wagers. Bets on one card were set on top of the card, while
bets on two cards were placed between them. The layout
measures 17" by 40".

Witherell's Americana Auctions

Early original gaming board.

"Steamboat" Cincinnati brand playing cards from the 1880s with authentic poker chips of the time.

Dennis Bailey

Card trimmer. Made of brass and steel with an ivory handle, this trimmer could be used legitimately to renew frayed edges , or illegitimately for shaving certain cards to make them easy to find in cutting the cards. Circa 1890.

Witherell's Americana Auctions

Another view of the card trimmer.

Witherell's Americana Auctions

Caille Brothers 50-cent Eclipse Upright Slot Machine with copper plated iron castings. The lower casting is of cupid kissing a damsel while cherubs and lion's paws form the legs. Circa 1900.

Witherell's Americana Auctions

Caille "Big Six" 25-cent upright slot machine. The action starts when a coin is dropped in one or all six slots, each slot's number corresponding to one on the wheel. Pushing down the lever on the coin head registers the bet, and pushing the front handles releases the notched wheel to spin. If the wheel stops on the number bet, the machine automatically pays out. Quarter sawn oak case, manufactured by the Caille Manufacturing Co., Michigan, circa 1900, measuring 70" by 26" by 16".

Witherell's Americana Auctions

Reliance Novelty Drop Card Poker Machine used to stimulate the sales of either drinks or cigars. For example, a royal flush awarded the player 100 cigars or drinks. Machines of this type were sometimes purchased by saloon proprietors, or more often they were placed by manufacturers on location where they were operated on a profit sharing basis. Manufactured in San Francisco, California, circa 1897, this was the earliest form of coin-operated gambling.

Witherell's Americana Auctions

Caille Brothers New Century Puck with music. In order to circumvent local gambling laws, the music box framed in the lower casing automatically plays a tune each time the machine is operated. Circa 1900.

Witherell's Americana Auctions

Sittman and Pitt "Little Model" card machine, the first coin-operated gambling machine to become nationally popular. Circa 1890.

Witherell's Americana Auctions

Cailles Silver Cup 5-cent slot machine. A rare and unusual machine with rotating dials. The corresponding colors on each dial must stop at the center arrow to pay out. Measures 20½" by 14", circa 1912.

Witherell's Americana Auctions

Keno Goose. A pivot-mounted device was spun to mix numbered balls within the central container from which they were withdrawn. Of all the games offered, Keno was the easiest game at which to cheat. It was played much like today's Bingo games. Manufactured by Will & Finch, San Francisco, California, circa 1890.

Witherell's Americana Auctions

Rare cast iron Mills Little Scarab with gum vendor. The mechanism of this machine is the same as the floor model Mills Roulette, with all the mechanism condensed into a counter model cabinet. The cabinet is decorated with dancing, busy scarab beetles. Very few scarab machines are known, and this is the only one known with a vendor. Measures 16" by 18", circa 1910.

Witherell's Americana Auctions

Abalone Mother-of-Pearl Gambling wheel. Eagles perched on American shields and lustrous mother-of-pearl decorate this unique wheel of fortune. Reverse painted on glass, abalone mother-of-pearl backed and nickel trim, measuring 84" by 50", circa 1900.

Witherell's Americana Auctions

Gambling horse race wheel with odds changer, manufactured by the Evans Co., Chicago, Illinois, complete with stand and top finial (not shown in the photo). Attractive reverse painted on glass horse race scenes surround the wheel. Circa 1900, measuring 88" by 60".

Witherell's Americana Auctions

Cast iron 1-cent match dispenser. Griffins guard the chute from which the lever releases match boxes from alternate columns. Circa 1910, measuring 14" by 6".

Witherell's Americana Auctions

Cast iron Duremus Cigar Dispenser, quite rare and highly desirable with the original marquee. Beveled throughout, original operating instructions below lever, high relief castings. Circa 1900, measuring 19" by 10".

Witherell's Americana Auctions

Rare cast iron Bull's Head Perfume Dispenser. Taking the bull by the horns causes him to snort perfume or cologne from his nostrils. manufactured by Continental Novelty Co., Buffalo, New York. Measures 16" by 18", circa 1904.

Witherell's Americana Auctions

Extremely rare Schilling, Stollwereck and Co's. Progressive Sampler 5-cent chocolate dispenser with clock. Unique clockwork mechanism dispenses chocolate when coin is inserted. Cased in elaborate Victorian-style cabinet with ornate ormolu attachments. The pedestal base is flanked with pilasters terminating at the scalloped roof-like structure with finials. The spring-driven clock strikes on the hour and the half hour, while a complicated clockwork mechanism dispenses the chocolate. Circa 1900, measuring 50" by 18½".

Witherell's Americana Auctions

Cast iron and pressed metal turtle spittoon. Stepping on the turtle's head raises the shell to expose the spittoon. Circa 1890, measuring 11" by 14".

Witherell's Americana Auctions

Beautiful National Saloon Cash Register, cast in bronze. This early example is considered the most ornate small model produced. Note the time clock mounted on the left side. Circa 1890.

Witherell's Americana Auctions

Label under glass back bar bottle of pretty lady, circa 1900.

Witherell's Americana Auctions

Label under glass flask with patriotic motif.

Witherell's Americana Auctions

A.D. Cooper, the premier western saloon artist, was a master at stirring the imaginations of saloon patrons. Here he depicts a scantily clad fallen angel in desperate need of help along the rugged California coastline.

Witherell's Americana Auctions

Inspired by George Catlin, A.D. Cooper often painted Indians as well as bar nudes. Here he depicts a wonderfully executed Indian warrior and his squaw in full regalia.

Witherell's Americana Auctions

Henry Raschen, a friend of Geronimo, portrayed the Arizona tribal life with great accuracy. This portrait is believed to be a rendering of Natches, a confidant of Geronimo and a fierce Indian chief.

Witherell's Americana Auctions

Edgar Samuel Paxson was one of the competent western artists to paint life in the West at the turn of the century. He not only portrayed the West with exhaustingly accurate detail, but also lived the life he depicted, among other things as an Indian scout, stage driver, and ranch hand.

Paxson, a native of Chicago, moved to Montana in 1877. He vowed never to return, stating: "I would not trade a weekend in Montana for a lifetime in Chicago."

Witherell's Americana Auctions

Chew Tomahawk Plug, paper board sign. Indians, Indians and more Indians on painter's palette. P. Lorillard & Co., Jersey City, New Jersey. Circa 1900, measuring 25" by 17".

Witherell's Americana Auctions

This self-framed tin advertising sign definitely portrays the cowboy's three pleasures in life: horses, women and whiskey, though not necessarily in that order!

Witherell's Americana Auctions

Die cut advertising calendar, circa 1908, with embossed cowgirl with vignette of horses. 21" by 11".

Witherell's Americana Auctions

Ruhstaller's Gilt Edge Beer, self-framed tin sign—a great work from an historic Sacramento brewery. Titled "The Cockfight," copyright 1912, American Art Works, Coshocton, Ohio. Measures 24" by 20".

Witherell's Americana Auctions

The "Double O" Cyrus Noble and W.A. Lacey Whiskies paper sign, Crown Distilleries Co., New York, San Francisco, Cincinnati, copyright 1910, Clarence M. Leavy. Shows gentlemen of the day wagering at the roulette table. Circa 1910, measuring 26" by 40".

Witherell's Americana Auctions

Zang Pilsener Beer glass sign, reverse painted on glass with a blue foil background. This sign comes from Denver, Colorado, made by F. Tochfarber Manufacturers, Cincinnati, Ohio, circa 1899. This rare sign measures 20" by 28".

Witherell's Americana Auctions

Union Brewing and Malting Co., embossed tin on cardboard sign, "We never disagree about the purity of Cascade Beer." A great San Francisco sign with Uncle Sam. Bachrach & Company, San Francisco, California. Circa 1900, measuring 17" by 21".

Witherell's Americana Auctions

Neef's reverse painted on glass advertising sign for Colorado Beer. Elaborate graphics on convex glass. Circa 1900.

Witherell's Americana Auctions

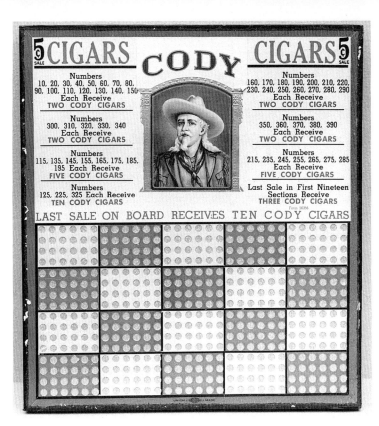

Old cigar punchboard, promoting the sale of Cody cigars. For 5 cents, the player punched out a number, and, depending upon the number, won from two to ten Cody cigars. 11⅜ by 10½ inches, printed in colors, primarily red, black and shades of yellow, the edges trimmed in black.

Richard A. Bourne Co., Inc.

Carved Frank Polk figure with Mill 10-cent Black Beauty Slot, a rare and highly important piece of American folk art, carved by Frank Polk in his own image. Frank Polk, the man, is not only a highly competent artist, but has also led an adventurous life as a rodeo rider, carousing cowboy, entertainer, dude wrangler, hollywood extra, and author of his own story, "F-F-F-Frank Polk" (He stutters).

As an artist, he is a respected member of the Rodeo Historical Society, the Cowboy Artists of America, and a western artist regarded as the dean of cowboy artists. Polk himself is somewhat more down to earth, calling himself a whittler. The manufacturing of the Frank Polk figures lasted but a few short years in the early 1950s. There are believed to be only six such figures remaining. Circa 1950, measuring 61" by 27".

Witherell's Americana Auctions

Cowboys, gentlemen, and gamblers, all carried pocket watches before the turn of the century. These watches are some of the finest and most expensive watches produced. Completely engraved and molded with multi-colored gold, they well portray the West with trains and horse racing.

Witherell's Americana Auctions

Regina coin-operated 1-cent music box, in a vertical format cased in oak, and, in this particular case, with exceptional tonal quality. Style 17A, duplex combs, manufactured by the Regina Music Box Co., Rahway, New Jersey. This rare piece comes with (10) 12¼" discs. Circa 1900, measuring 20" by 19".

Witherell's Americana Auctions

Coin-operated Regina 27" Disc Orchestral Music Box, originally retailed by Wise Piano House, Walla Walla, Washington. This coin-operated Regina Music Box is one of the most impressive styles ever made by the company in Rahway, New Jersey. Circa 1900, measuring 78" by 45".

Witherell's Americana Auctions

The centerpiece of any great saloon! Coin operated Regina "Suprema" Disc Music Box. This 5-cent coin operated musical marvel was the forerunner of today's juke box. Oak case, circa 1895.

Witherell's Americana Auctions

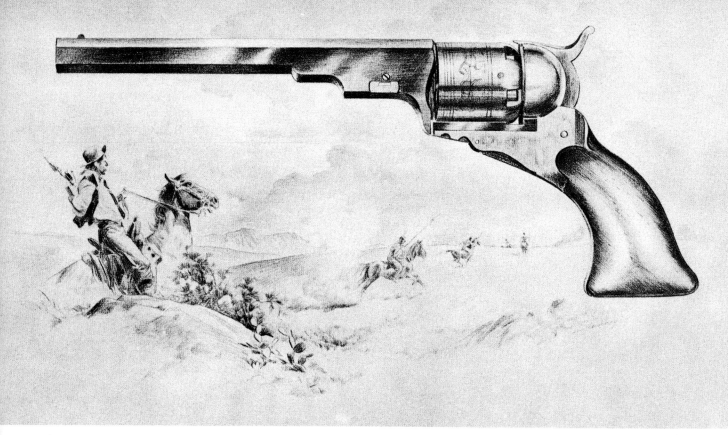

Colt Texas Paterson .40 caliber—1836. The Colt Texas Paterson was the famous revolver that helped Texas win its independence and statehood in its war with Mexico. Manufactured in Samuel Colt's first plant at Paterson, New Jersey, from 1836 to 1841, it was the first successful revolver to be produced on a mass production basis.

The Texas Paterson fired five .40 caliber rounded bullets. A combination bullet and powder flask was used that loaded five measured charges of powder into the chambers at once from one end and placed five round bullets simultaneously into the chambers from the other end. The percussion primers were fed from a magazine capping device.

A small front sight was let into the barrel and a notch was cut in the top of the hammer to form a rear sight when the revolver was cocked and ready to fire.

The revolver had a plain blued finish with an ornamental design engraved on the cylinder, an octagonal shaped barrel, and no ramrod. It was furnished in different barrel lengths with regular or straight stocks. It had a folding trigger but no trigger guard.

Colt Patent Firearms, Inc.

Opposite page top:

Colt Walker Model .44 caliber—1847. The Whineyville Walker Colt, or Model of 1847 Army Pistol, was a strong and powerful six-shot .44 caliber weapon, weighing four pounds, nine ounces. It was developed with the help of Captain Sam Walker of the Texas Rangers and saw service in the Mexican War. In contrast to the Colt Texas Paterson, it had a trigger guard and a loading lever. Dispensing with the folding Paterson type of trigger, it had a regular trigger with a brass, square back trigger guard and strap combined.

A jointed lever ramrod was attached to the underside of the barrel to seat the conical or round bullets correctly in the chambers of the cylinder. Barrel length was nine inches, the overall length, 15½ inches. Sights were blade and hammer notch.

This impressive weapon, the heaviest gun in the history of the Colt revolver, was sometimes known as the First Dragoon Model.

Colt Patent Firearms, Inc.

Opposite page bottom:

Colt Wells Fargo Model .31 caliber—1848. In the days of winning the West, the Wells Fargo Express Company, which played an important part in opening up new frontiers, armed its guards and riders against highwaymen and Indians with the gun that has become identified with the company's name. Although some dispute has centered about the correct model, Colt feels that the gun bearing the Wells Fargo name in their set of prints is the authoritative one.

The Wells Fargo Model illustrated was a five shot weapon of .31 caliber, without a ramrod, and with an octagonal barrel six inches long. It had a square back trigger guard and brass pin and hammer notch sights.

This model, with three inch barrel, was also known as the Model of 1848 Pocket Pistol and is sometimes called the Baby Dragoon.

Colt's Patent Firearms, Inc.

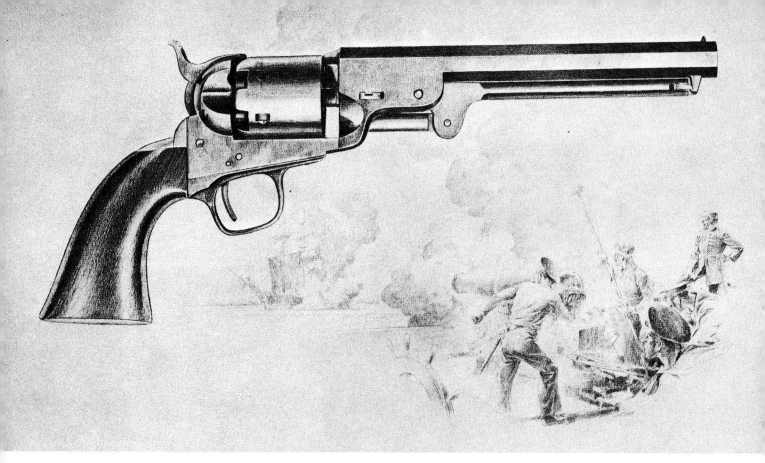

Colt Navy Model .36 caliber—1851. The Colt Navy Pistol, also known as the Model of 1851 Navy Pistol or the Old Model Navy Pistol, was a .36 caliber weapon with a six-shot cylinder and a seven and one-half inch octagonal barrel. It is identified by caliber and the usual naval battle scene engraved around the cylinder.

Designed for warfare at sea, the Navy Model was also a very popular arm for use as a belt revolver, being handier and lighter than the Dragoon, its predecessor. It was also a favorite dueling weapon in California during the 1850s. It was sometimes referred to as the Old Model Belt Pistol.

It had a hinged lever ramrod, took a conical bullet, and weighed two pounds, ten ounces. It was equipped with a Navy latch and an iron trigger guard. Commercial models were generally equipped with a brass trigger guard.

Colt's Patent Firearms, Inc.

Opposite page top:

Colt Army Model .44 caliber—1860. The Model of 1860 Army Revolver, or the Round Barreled Army Revolver, was the largest of a new series of revolvers which Colt put on the market about 1860. This arm was a .44 caliber six-shot revolver made on the same frame as the Model of 1851 Navy Revolver, but with a rebated cylinder large enough to accommodate the .44 caliber bullet.

The Army Model was the principal revolver used by the Northern Army during the Civil War. It came in two barrel lengths, seven and one-half and eight inches. Its weight averaged two pounds, eleven ounces and it was a much handier gun that the heavy Dragoon that it superseded. The regular model was cut for shoulder stock, but some were made to order without the cut. Special lots were also turned out with rebated fluted cylinders.

The barrel, cut short at the rounded section of the breech to allow for extra length in the cylinder, was round in its entire length and fitted with a creeping lever ramrod. The gun was manufactured from 1860 to 1872.

Colt's Patent Firearms, Inc.

Opposite page bottom:

Colt Peacemaker .45 caliber—1873. The Colt Peacemaker or Single Action Army Revolver is the traditional arm of the Old West. When new frontiers were blazed, the Peacemaker helped protect the settlers against hostile Indians and wild animals. It is closely linked with the romantic sagas of frontier days, when Buffalo Bill, Wild Bill Hickok, Wyatt Earp, Billy the Kid, and Calamity Jane dispensed what was known as "Colt justice."

The Peacemaker was the first large revolver made by Colt to use self-exploding cartridges. It had a six-shot cylinder chambered for a .45 caliber center fire cartridge and came in different barrel lengths: seven and one-half inches, or cavalry model; five and one-half inches, or artillery model; and four and three-quarters inches, or civilian model. The .44 caliber model was known as the Frontier Model.

The Peacemaker manufactured today is essentially the same gun that it was when first produced over 120 years ago. It has been chambered for different sizes of cartridges and is a favorite everywhere.

Colt's Patent Firearms, Inc.

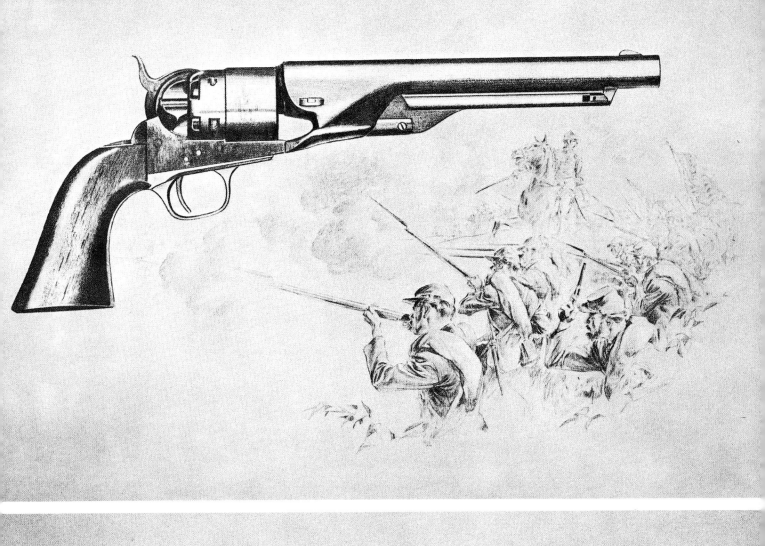
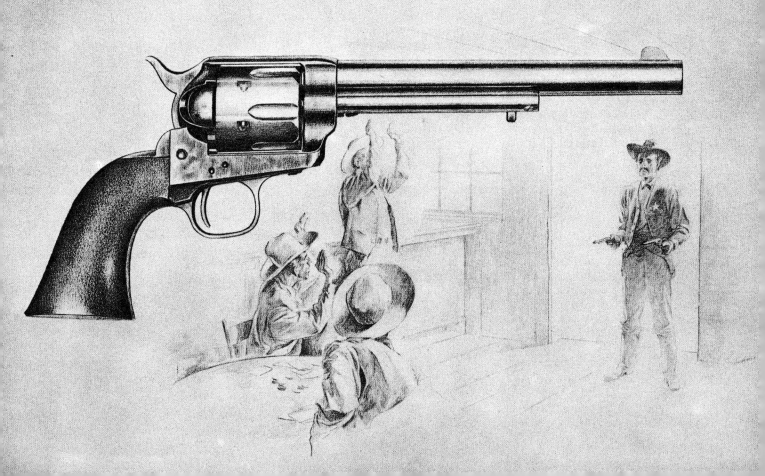

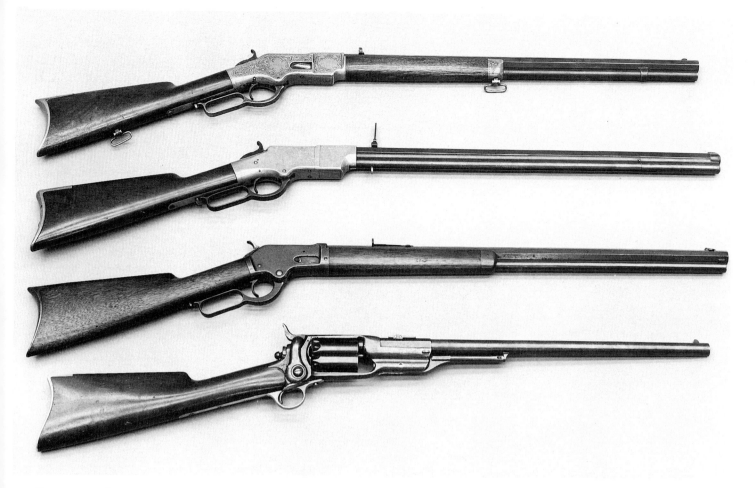

From top to bottom:

Factory engraved Winchester Model 1866 Rifle, Serial number 39567. With 24 inch octagonal barrel, full magazine, the forend cap and top of the buttplate factory scroll engraved, the frame fully factory scroll-engraved, with unusually heavy coverage leaving the two panels in the pattern on each side of the frame, most likely for some presentation inscriptions which were never done. Fitted with the original deluxe walnut stocks and sling swivels.

Civil War Henry Repeating Rifle, serial number 3171. Fitted with original sling swivel on the left side of the butt and sling swivel ring on the left side of the barrel.

Colt-Burgess Lever Action Rifle, serial number 8139. With 25½ inch octagonal barrel and full magazine.

Scarce and Highly Collectible Colt Root Model 1855 Saddle Ring Carbine. Caliber .56 with 21 inch barrel, stamped "Colt's Patent" on the left side of the frame. It has a heavy saddle ring stud and ring, brass trigger guard and buttplate. The oil finished walnut buttstock is stamped on the left side in large letters: "J. Prie & Cie/ANVERS."

Richard A. Bourne Co., Inc.

Detail picture of the factory-engraved Winchester Model 1866 rifle.

Richard A. Bourne Co., Inc.

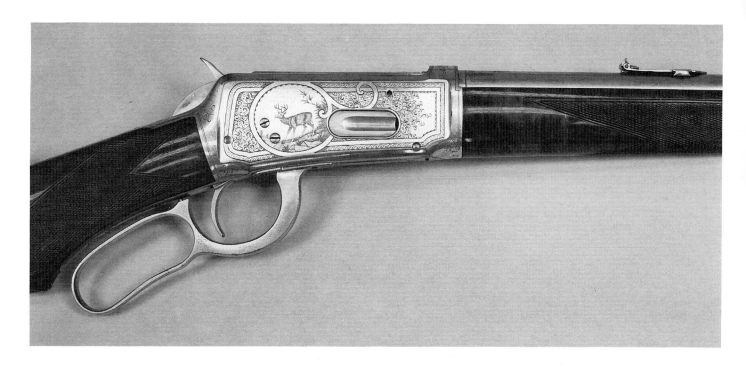

Model 1894 Winchester caliber 30 WCF Sample Gun, serial number 128249. Full factory scroll engraved, the left side with a large panel showing a ram, the right side with a stag, light scroll work at the rear of the round barrel, a bit more on the forend cap, very deluxe varnished wood with "WINCHESTER," etc. checkered hard rubber shotgun butt plate. This rifle was first shipped from the warehouse on March 10, 1904, it then spent almost 24 years being shipped to various exhibitions and dealers as a "sample consignment," the last recorded entry being dated January 4, 1928. A superb and historically important Winchester that would be suitable for any collection.

Richard A. Bourne Co., Inc.

Left side view if the Winchester Sample Gun.

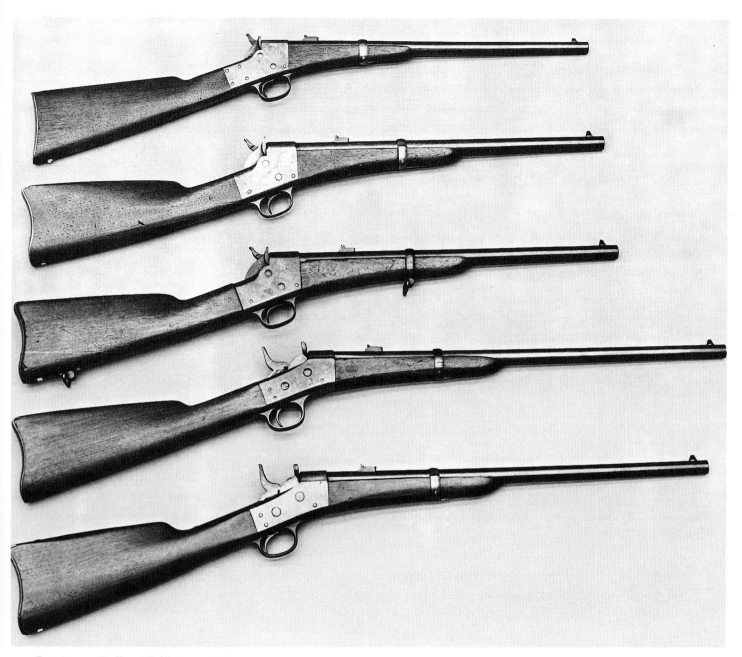

Remington Rolling Block Action rifles, from top to bottom:

1. Remington split breech saddle ring carbine, .46 caliber. Martially marked overall, with two script cartouche inspection marks, "CGC" and "TB".

2. Remington split breech military carbine, .50 caliber. Fitted with saddle ring and bar on the left side, the butt plate stamped "US."

3. Remington split breech saddle ring carbine, .50 caliber. Variation fitted with sling swivel mounted on the front.

The barrel band and rear sling swivel inset at the bottom of the butt stock, with the butt plate stamped "US."

4. Remington Naval Contract Rolling Block carbine, caliber .50-70. Fitted with a 23¼ inch barrel, serial no. 4729 and struck with the Naval anchor.

5. Remington New York State Contract Saddle Ring Carbine, caliber .50-70, the left side of the stock stamped "TROUP 'C' N.Y." 22 inch barrel with saddle ring and side bar.

Richard A. Bourne Co., Inc.

Colt Gatling Gun, serial no. 27, caliber .30 with ten 28 inch enclosed steel barrels. Fitted with the M. 1883 style cocking switch, the firing crank fitted to the right side for gear reduced firing can also very quickly be mounted at the rear of the casing for firing direct drive for a higher cyclic rate of fire. This particular model is unusual for the fact that the casing covers the muzzles of the upper half of the barrels. This weapon incorporates the hopper for the Bruce feed system. Notice how well-fitted are the ammo and parts boxes to the mount, making a compact unit able to be handled by the fewest men possible. Weapons such as this were used by the Army in its campaigns against dissident Indian tribes on the frontier.

Richard A. Bourne Corp., Inc.

Front view of the Gatling Gun, showing how the muzzles of the upper barrels are covered by the casing.

Richard A. Bourne Co., Inc.

Detail of the Gatling Gun plate.

Richard A. Bourne Co., Inc.

Remington New Model Army .44 caliber revolver, serial
number 201xx.

Mac Mechensturm

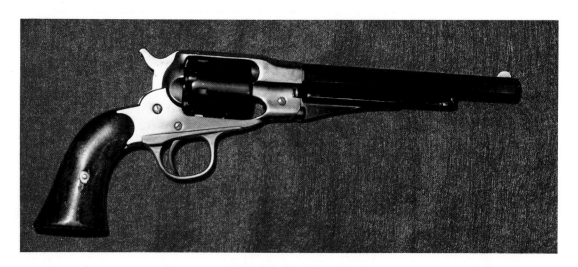

Remington New Model Police .36 caliber revolver, serial
number 140xx.

Mac Mechensturm

Manhattan .36 caliber Model revolver, serial number 5xx.

Mac Mechensturm

Colt Army Model 1860 .44 caliber revolver, manufactured
in 1861. Serial number 160xx.

Mac Mechensturm

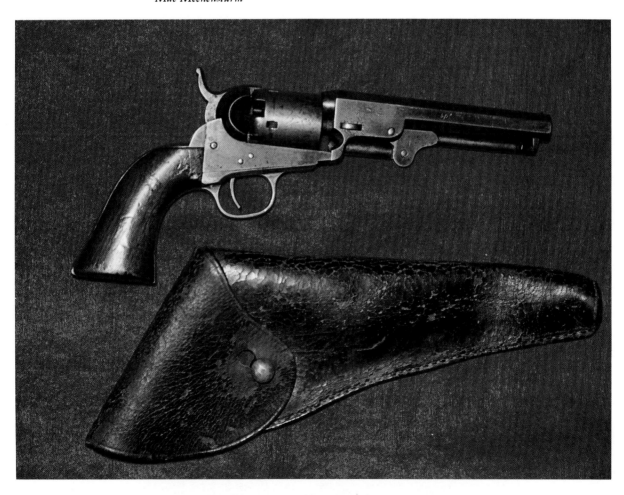

1849 Colt Pocket Model .36 caliber revolver. Note the 5
inch barrel and the original full flap holster. This pistol was
manufactured in 1855. Serial number 1295xx.

Mac Mechensturm

Colt .38 caliber rimfire revolver with 3½ inch round barrel. Note the absence of an ejector. Made in 1873, serial number 29xx.

Mac Mechensturm

Colt Lightning Double Action .41 caliber revolver with 6 inch barrel, serial number 1307xx. This piece was manufactured in 1901.

Mac Mechensturm

Colt 1902 .45 caliber Alaskan/Philippine Model revolver, serial number 469xx. When the Colt .38 proved to have insufficient stopping power in the Moro pacification, the Army was called upon to ship the Alaskan Model in .45 caliber to the Philippines. This proved to be the answer to "Juramentado."

Mac Mechensturm

Colt 1892 New Army/Navy .38 caliber revolver, serial number 1106xx. This weapon was manufactured in 1899.

Mac Mechensturm

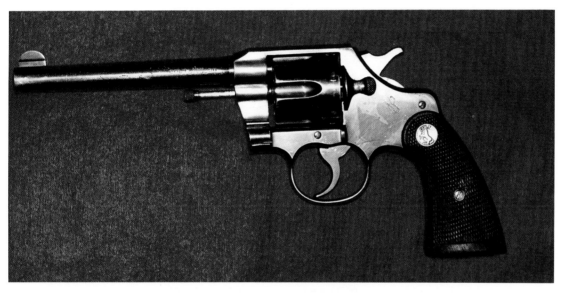

Colt Army Special Model, .38 Special, serial number 5227xx.

#ST2Mac Mechensturm

New Pocket Model Double Action .32 caliber Colt revolver, serial number 69xx. this particular pistol was produced in 1895.

Mac Mechensturm

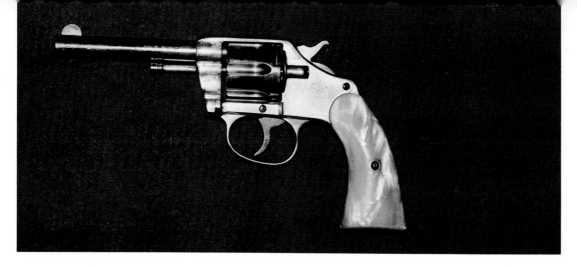

Colt New Police Model .32 caliber revolver, serial number 41xx, manufactured in 1898. This weapon has the original pearl grips.

Mac Mechensturm

Colt New Police Model .32NP caliber revolver, serial number 262xx. This weapon was produced in 1904.

Mac Mechensturm

Colt New Police Positive .32NP caliber revolver, serial number 532xx.

Mac Mechensturm

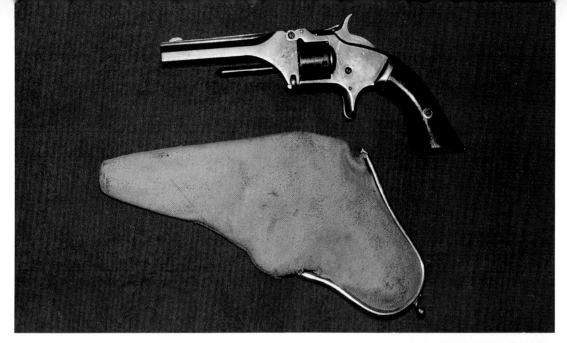

Smith and Wesson Model Number 1, second issue .22 caliber revolver manufactured in 1866, serial number 602xx. Note the original purse-closure carrying case.

Mac Mechensturm

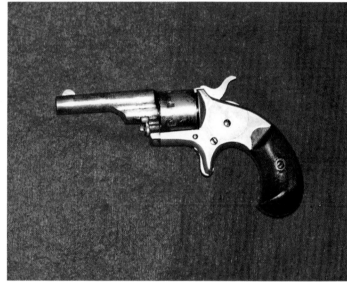

Colt Open Top Pocket Model .22 caliber revolver, serial number 1135xx. This weapon was made in 1877.

Mac Mechensturm

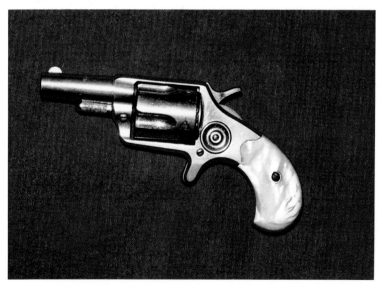

Colt New Line .38 caliber rim fire revolver, serial number 3xx. Manufactured in 1874. Note the original pearl grips.

Mac Mechensturm

Colt New Line .22 caliber revolver, serial number 169xx.
This particular piece was made in 1876.

Mac Mechensturm

Remington .41 caliber Double Derringer, serial number
1xx. A good back-up weapon often found in the West.

Mac Mechensturm

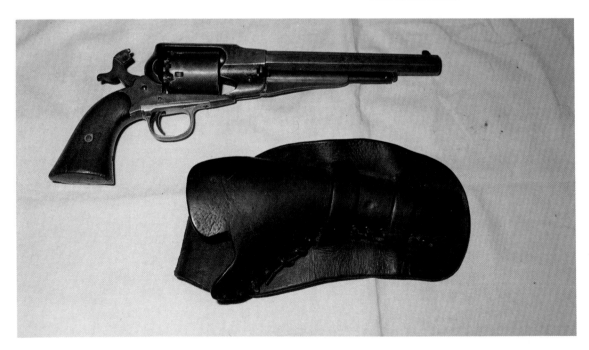

Remington .44 caliber revolver with brass trigger guard,
accompanied by a rawhide laced double loop Mexican loop
holster.

Dennis Bailey

Exhibition Colt S.A. Serial No. 206340, caliber 38WCF, 5½ inch barrel, with modern scroll engraving overall and fitted with custom engraved Mexican sterling silver grips with gold overlay including a gold plaque on each side engraved "E.W." for "Eddie West," former Hollywood stuntman and producer and star of a fancy gun and trick shooting act. The tooled black leather with brass tack decoration cowboy cuffs were made by Wyeth Hardware & Mfg. Co., St. Joseph, Missouri.

Richard A. Bourne Co., Inc.

Colt Single Action Revolver, serial number 87. An extremely rare and desirable "pinched frame" early production revolver. The barrel has seven-groove gain-twist rifling, which was used only on the earliest produced single actions. This one of only 15 known examples of the Colt single action with serial number lower than 100.

Richard A. Bourne Co., Inc.

Top view of Colt Single Action revolver.

Richard A. Bourne Co., Inc.

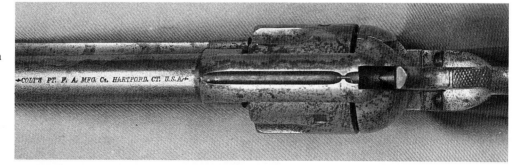

Bottom view of Colt Single Action revolver.

Richard A. Bourne Co., Inc.

Unique Western Colt Single Action 7½ inch barrel .44-40 Revolver, serial # 165577. The frame of this pistol is fitted with the large stud screw for attaching to the L.S. Flatau Patent pistol and carbine holder. Complete with the original cartridge belt with the Flatau holder manufactured by Bridgeport G.I. Co., the brown leather belt with a fancy rectangular buckle embossed with different patterns.

Richard A. Bourne Co.,Inc.

Factory engraved Colt Single Action Army revolver, serial no. 75137/2, profusely engraved overall with a very tight scroll pattern by Gustave Young. The engraving includes the rear of the cylinder and the flat part of the loading lever, fitted with the very rare original panel checkered and carved one-piece burl walnut grips. It is in the original walnut Colt Army case lined with maroon velvet, complete with a "COLTS/PATENT" Army flask embossed on one side only, a steel "COLTS/PATENT" bullet mold, correct nipple wrench screw driver, a tin of "ELEY" caps for Colt, and a packet of paper cartridges.

Richard A. Bourne Co., Inc.

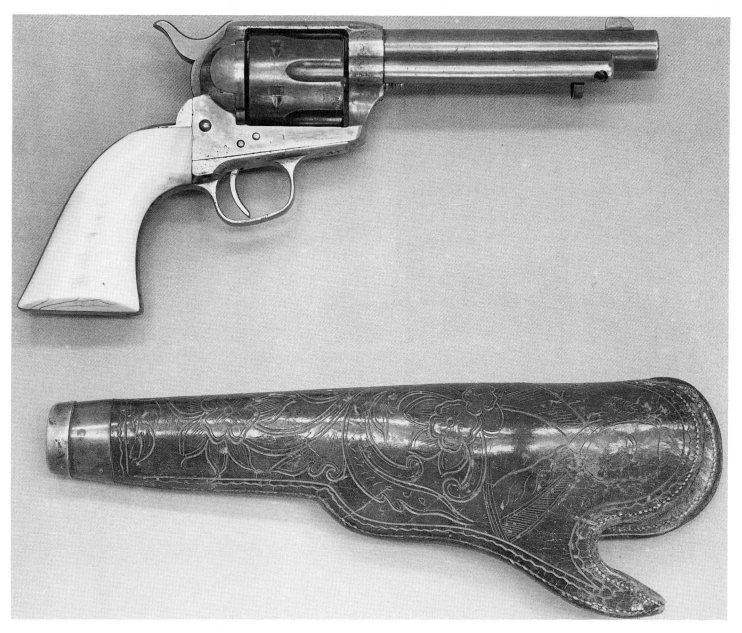

Inscribed Colt Single Action .45 caliber 7½" barrel revolver, serial number 43247. The backstrap is inscribed in script "B.N. Waters, U.S.A.," one of the first inscribed single action revolvers made by Colt. This pistol was part of the first shipment of record of a lot of six, shipped 1 July 1878 to a T.F. Swain. All of the backstraps were inscribed to officers of the 15th Infantry Regiment stationed at Fort Wingate, New Mexico, then campaigning against the Apaches.

A great Gallatin holster for a Colt model 1860 Army revolver. The leather is embossed with a large bust portrait of George Washington on the upper portion, while the balance of the leather is tooled in a floral pattern. The tip of the holster has a heavy silver fitting drilled with a .45" diameter hole in the bottom for drainage. The interior is lined with a deep red morocco leather, while the belt loop is marked E L GALLATIN & CO/ MAKERS DENVER.

Richard A. Bourne Co., Inc.

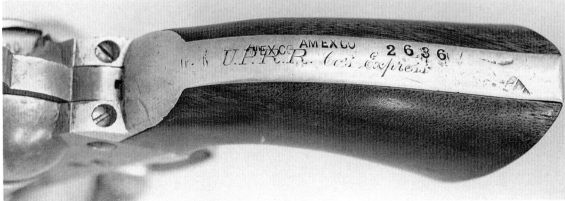

Rare Colt Model 1871 .44 caliber rimfire Open Top revolver, serial number 421 with Navy size grips and brass straps. The backstrap has the original engraved inscription "U.P.R.R. Co's Express" (Union Pacific Rail Road) and a period die struck marking "AMEXCO 2636" (American Express Co.) above this inscription, with a partial striking of "MEXICO" struck on the upper curve of the backstrap and intermingled with the first markings. This pistol is verified as original by the Union Pacific Railroad.

Below is a rare converted Model 1861 Colt revolver, serial number 2566/1, all matching. This is a very rare variation with iron trigger guard and brass backstrap. Note that the right side of the one piece grip is carved with the Mexican eagle.

Richard A. Bourne Co., Inc

Six pistols found on the frontier, top to bottom and left to right:

Remington New Model Police revolver with a rare 6½ inch barrel, serial number 7156. This was a factory conversion to .38 caliber rimfire.

A rare Colt Lightning revolver with 4½ inch barrel in .32 caliber, serial number 74464.

A Pacific Express Co. Model 1877 4½ inch barrel .38 caliber Colt revolver, serial number 143401. The backstrap has the original markings "PAC.EX.CO.143401."

Smith and Wesson Volcanic pistol in .30 caliber, with the small frame, serial number E45.

Smith and Wesson .38 caliber single action 2nd model revolver with 5 inch barrel.

Cooper Navy model revolver with 4 inch barrel. This is the second model with rebated cylinder

Richard A. Bourne Co., Inc.

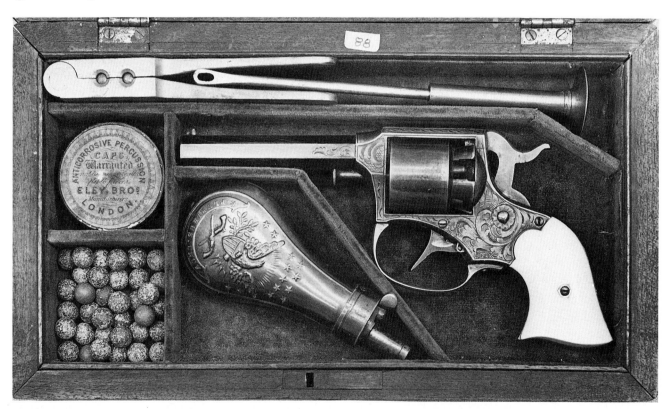

Cased Remington-Rider percussion revolver, serial no. 6382. An extremely rare factory-engraved version with scroll engraving about the barrel address. The frame is profusely scroll-engraved including the backstrap and butt, and the trigger guard also has engraved decoration. Fitted with original ivory grips. It is in its original fitted walnut case, with all accessories.

Richard A. Bourne Co., Inc.

Remington Iroquois pocket revolver, the round cylinder variation. These were made circa 1878-1888. It is in its original lined walnut case.

Richard A. Bourne Co., Inc.

Union Metallic Cartridge Co. Display Board. This cartridge board typifies the rather extravagant and effective lengths to which companies would go in promoting their products during the 19th century. Circa 1890, measuring 41″ by 55″.

Witherell's Americana Auctions

UMC Lithograph Cartridge Board Poster, Lindener, Eddy and Clauss, Lith. N.Y. A rare cartridge board poster, produced by the Union Metallic Cartridge Co. of Bridgeport, Connecticut, depicting the American fleet at sea. Circa 1890, measuring 30" by 44".

Witherell's Americana Auctions

Winchester "Double W" cartridge board, the most famous and well known cartridge board produced by Winchester. The "Double W" board is both the largest and most complicated made, with a total of 182 cartridges. Circa 1897, measuring 40" by 57" including the original frame.

Witherell's Americana Auctions

The most sought-after Winchester Cartridge Board. The single "W" was by far the most elaborate board produced by the Winchester Cartridge Company. Circa 1890.

Witherell's Americana Auctions

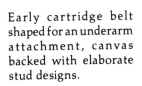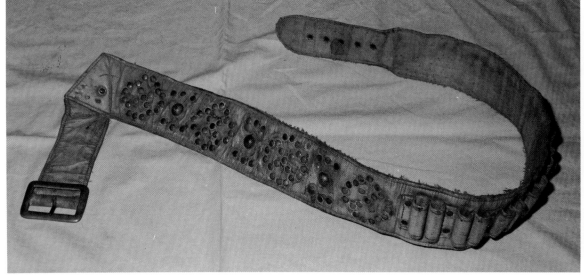

Early cartridge belt shaped for an underarm attachment, canvas backed with elaborate stud designs.

Dennis Bailey

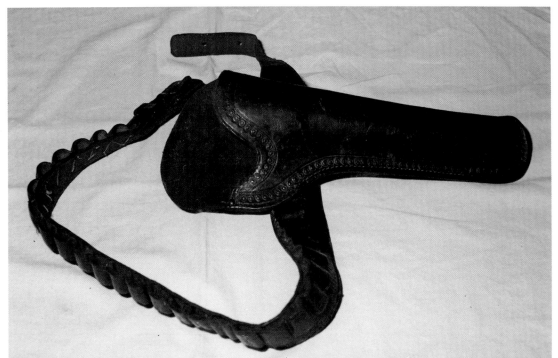

Very early Slim Jim style leather holster, the back marked "5-7½" for barrel length, while the holster is marked "KNX." The cartridge loop belt appears to be buffalo hide.

Dennis Bailey

Mexican-style double loop holster with padded belt. The back is marked with a reverse "R" to the left of a regular "R."

Dennis Bailey

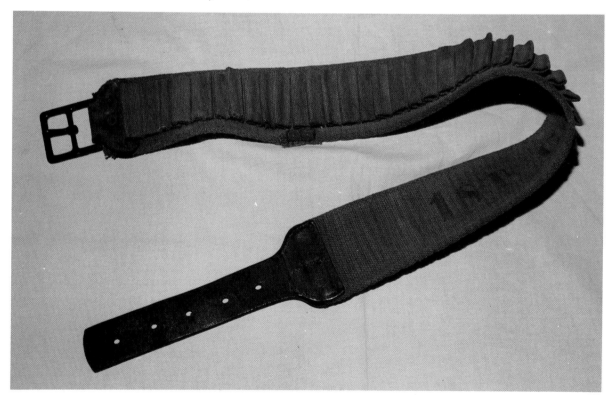

Indian War period military cartridge belt, marked 1st Cavalry.

Dennis Bailey

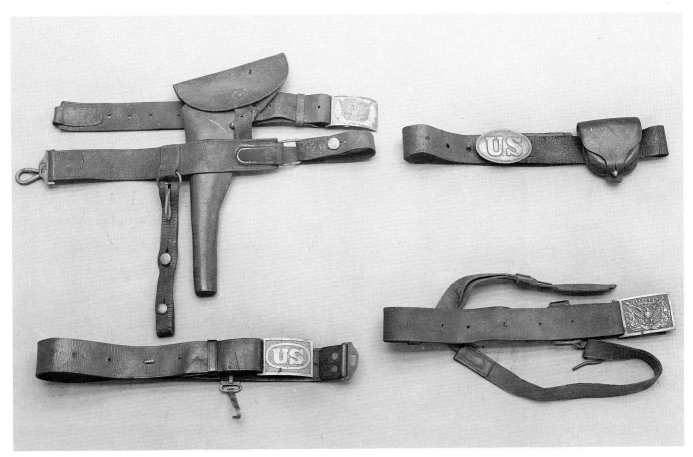

Top to bottom, left to right:

1. Civil War Officer-style belt, holster, sword carrying straps, with ornate rectangular brass buckle with applied silver wreath. This style was carried by the army throughout the days of the Indian Wars.

2. Indian Wars belt, with rectangular brass buckle with raised oval and "US". This particular specimen is stamped inside the belt with "1/13 CAV/7" and "35B 1."

3. Civil War issue belt, lead backed oval brass enlisted man's belt plate with the original black leather belt and "US" marked black leather cap box, stamped "JEWELL/MAKER/HARTFORD." This style was used well into the 1880s.

4. Civil War Officer's belt with rectangular brass plate with applied silvered wreath, as used for many years after the War.

Richard A. Bourne Co., Inc.

Opposite page top:

From top to bottom, left to right:

1. Western cartridge belt, brown leather, 3 inches wide, with loops for forty .44 or .45 caliber cartridges. Made of doubled over leather stitched on one edge, with a heavy 2¼ inch nickel plated buckle. Circa 1890.

2. Tooled western Colt SA holster of brown leather.

3. Colt M.1851 KM holster, made for the Austrian Kreigs Marine Colt Navies, designed for the pistol with a pouch for the spare cylinder to the side and another pouch in the front for the capper. Brown leather. Made for overseas sale, but found once in a great while out west.

4. Colt M.1851 KM holster, but missing the spare cylinder pouch.

5. Holster for a Colt M.1849 revolver, brown leather, made for the 6 inch barrel Colt Pocket Model.

6. Early holster made for what appears to be a Colt Navy.

Richard A. Bourne Co., Inc.

Opposite page bottom:

From left to right, top to bottom:

1. Embossed western style holster, for Colt New Service revolver with 7½ inch barrel. Single loop, Mexican style, 12½ inches overall, circa 1900.

2. Single loop Mexican style holster. A 5½ inch Colt SA fits fine. Circa 1900.

3. Triple loop Mexican style holster, 10½ inches in length, with light tooling.

4. Large embossed single loop Mexican style holster.

5. Heavily embossed flap closure holster, most likely for the New Service revolver.

6. Early embossed open top holster, cut for the guard.

Richard A. Bourne Co., Inc.

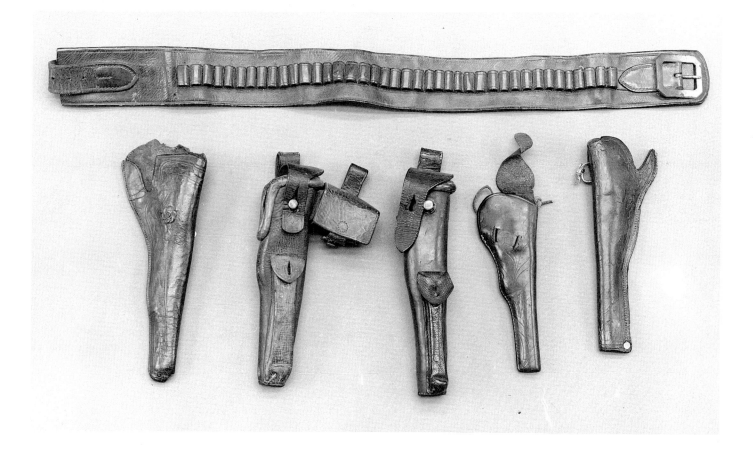

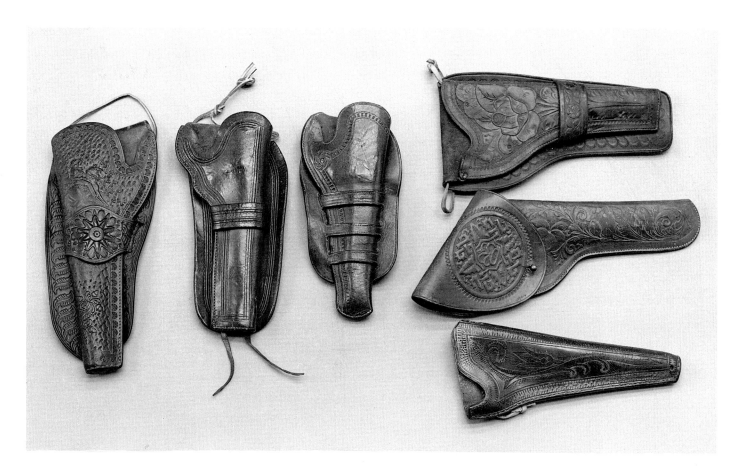

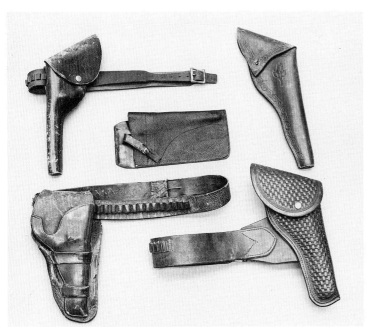

From left to right, top to bottom:

1. Flapped holster for .38 caliber DA revolver, possibly a Colt Model 1903, with an old belt with loops for .32 caliber cartridges.

2. Rectangular black pigskin holster, belt hung, but fitting in pocket, for a medium frame DA revolver.

3. Flapped holster for a large frame DA revolver with long barrel, heavily tooled overall.

4. Western style rig for a Colt New Service revolver, with loops for .38 caliber cartridges.

5. Flapped holster for Colt New Service revolver, the belt with loops for .38 caliber cartridges.

Richard A. Bourne Co., Inc.

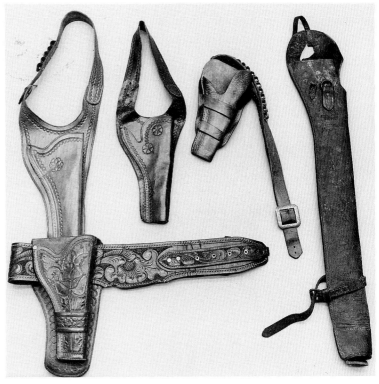

From left to right, top to bottom:

1. Leather shoulder holster, embossed, for a Colt SA or a medium frame DA revolver. The strap has loops for five .38 caliber cartridges.

2. Old tooled leather shoulder holster for a medium frame DA revolver.

3. Holster for a 5½ SA, with thin brown leather belt with loops for .38 caliber cartridges. Circa 1900.

4. 27 inch old rifle scabbard, circa 1890.

5. Fancy tooled leather western holster and rig for a large frame DA revolver, probably a Colt New Service.

Richard A. Bourne Co., Inc.

From left to right, top to bottom:

1. Typical western holster, circa 1885 for the 7½ inch SAA revolver, complete with original belt.

2. Another holster for a 7½ inch barrel SAA, with three thongs securing the holster to its backing with each having its own brass buckle. Loops for 32 cartridges.

3. Single Mexican loop for the 7½ inch SA, heavily tooled with a fancy pattern, the belt marked "W.WELLMAN/ MONT./WHITE SULPHER SPRINGS."

4. Holster and rig for a 4¾ inch Colt SA revolver, two rows of cartridge loops, one row .45, the other .38 caliber.

5. Old western policeman's belt, holster and billy club, circa 1895, the holster for a Colt Police Positive or similar size revolver.

Richard A. Bourne Co., Inc.

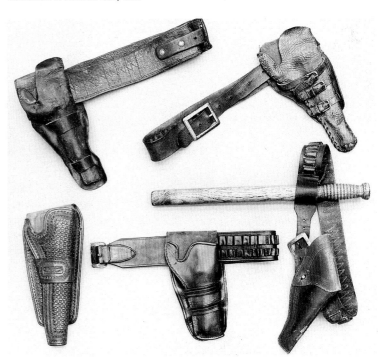

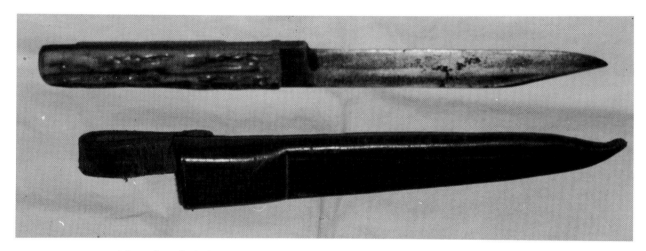

Horn-handled throwing and skinning knife, with original sheath.

Dennis Bailey

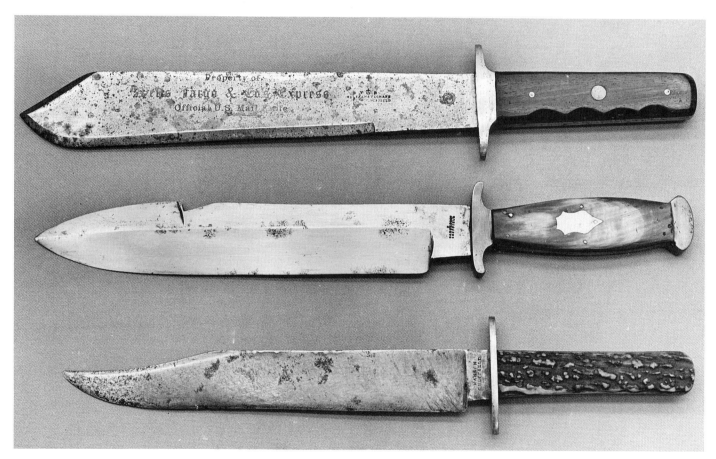

From top to bottom:

1. Unusual knife 16 inches overall with 10¾ inch blade, the reverse stamped "V (crown) R/MALEHAM & YEOMANS/ CUTLERY SHEFFIELD" and etched "Property of/Wells Fargo & Co.'s Express/Official U.S./Mail Knife," with German silver guard and plain wooden scales cut with finger grooves.

2. Rare and unusual antique knife 15¼ inches overall with 10⅛ inch blade stamped on the ricasso "F/BARNES & Co

SHEFFIELD." The back of the blade is cut with a notch 3½ inches from the tip, the hilt has a thick German silver pommel and guard, and is fitted with horn scales, one scale with elaborate shield-shaped inlay.

3. Nineteenth century Bowie-style knife, 14½ inches overall with 9⅝ inch blade stamped on the ricasso "MANSON/SHEFFIELD," fitted with plain German silver guard and natural staghorn scales.

Richard A. Bourne Co., Inc.

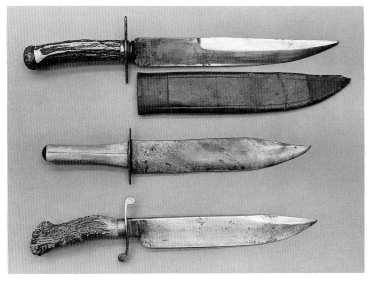

From top to bottom:

1. Nineteenth Century Bowie-style knife, 17½ inches overall with 11½ inch blade stamped on the left side "AUSTIN/MADURYHOZARY/... TCHINOPOI." The hilt with an iron guard and ferrule, with solid staghorn handle with round silver pommel embossed with a relief leaf decoration, complete with original brown leather scabbard.

2. Antique Bowie-style knife, 14½ inches overall with 10 inch wrought iron blade, primitively made, the hilt with wrought iron guard and round wrought iron pommel with solid bone grip.

3. Old large hunting knife, 15½ inches overall with 10⅜ inch blade stamped at the ricasso "HASSAM. BROTHERS/ BOSTON." The hilt has an S-shaped iron guard with natural antler horn grip with German silver ferrule at the guard and small round German silver pommel.

Richard A. Bourne Co., Inc.

From top to bottom:

1. Bowie knife, with 9 inch spear point blade marked on the ricasso
"✝ XL," the left side of the blade signed "WOLSTENHOLM & SON/WASHINGTON WORKS/SHEFFIELD," the hilt with reverse curved German silver guard fitted with plain wood scales.

2. Bowie knife with 7 inch double-edged spear point blade stamped on the ricasso "MANSON/SHEFFIELD," lightly etched on one side with a very large panel with some scrolling floral decoration and a ribbon "A SURE DEFENSE," fitted with the original fancy German silver hilt , in the original morocco leather scabbard with gold tooling and German silver throat and tip.

3. Bowie knife with 8 inch single-edge spear point blade struck on the ricasso "MANSON/SHEFFIELD," the blade etched on one side with a large panel with a ribbon "THE GOLD SEEKERS PROTECTOR." Fitted with a fancy original German silver hilt. In the original light green morocco leather scabbard with gold tooling, German silver throat and tip.

Richard A. Bourne Co., Inc.

From top to bottom:

1. Massive antique Bowie knife, 19⅝ inches overall with 13½ inch heavy blade. The back of the blade almost ½ inches wide! Fitted with a heavy brass guard and heavy brass cast grip with a snake wrapped all the way around the grip biting the skull pommel.

2. Bowie knife, 17 inches overall with 12¼ inch blade stamped on the left hand side "AUSTIN." It has a wrought iron guard and staghorn grip with floral embossed silver ferrule at the guard and large floral embossed silver pommel, the very top of which is engraved with a coat of arms.

3. Antique Bowie knife, 14 inches overall with 9¼ inch blade stamped at the ricasso "J.ROGERS & SONS/No 6 NORFOLK St/SHEFFIELD." The hilt has a German silver guard with ball finials fitted with staghorn scales. In the original brown leather scabbard with German silver tip and throat.

Richard A. Bourne Co., Inc.

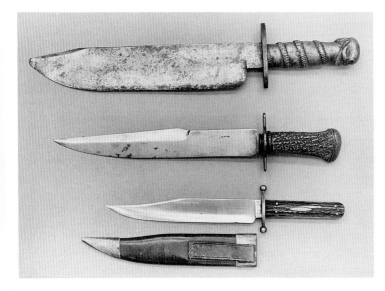

From left to right:

Rodgers 11¾ inch knife with 7 inch blade deeply stamped "J. Rodgers & SONS/No.6 NORFOLK St/Sheffield," German silver crossguard with ball tips, black horn scales secured by 5 German silver rivets, in an antique heavy leather scabbard not original to the knife.

Rodgers 10⅜ inch knife with 6¼ inch blade deeply stamped "J. RODGERS & SONS/No. 6 NORFOLK St/SHEFFIELD," German silver crossguard with ball finials, black horn scales secured by 5 rivets, in the original leather scabbard with German silver mounts.

Small Bowie knife, 10⅛ inches overall, the 5⅞ inch blade deeply stamped "L.F. & G." at the ricasso, heavy German silver crossguard, staghorn scales held with four brass rivets, dates from the second half of the 19th Century.

Unusual Rodgers knife , 10¼ inches overall, the 5¾ inch blade stamped "JOSEPH RODGERS/ & SONS.

SHEFFIELD," nickel plated curved steel crossguard, German silver ferrule, the bone grip with fluted carving at the pommel, complete with the original scabbard with German silver throat and tip, the body a celluloid type material that looks very much like ivory.

Lady's Dirk, 83/16 inches overall, the 5 inch double edged blade, coin silver crossguard and ferrule, ivory grip with silver cap for the blade tang, in the original brown morocco leather scabbard with silver throat and tip, c. 1825—1850, probably American.

Lady's Dirk, 8 inches overall with a 4½ inch double edged blade with heavy median ridge, coin silver crossguard and ferrule, turned bone hilt with flattened sides, the pommel with a coin silver plate that holds the blade tang, complete with the original red morocco leather scabbard , c. 1825 1850, probably American.

Richard A. Bourne Co., Inc.

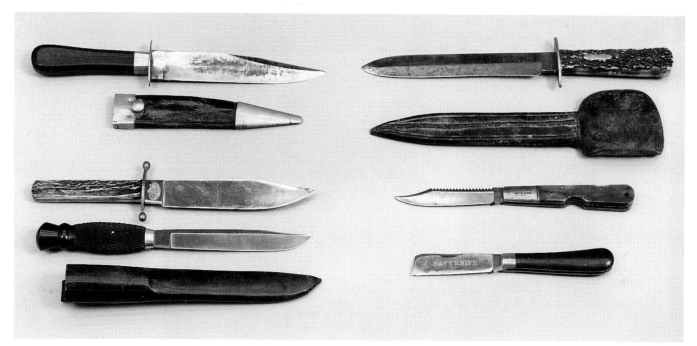

From left to right, top to bottom:

Russell Bowie knife with 7" blade stamped in two ribbons "J. Russell & Co." and "Green River Works," German silver crossguard and ferrule, rosewood handle in the original black leather scabbard.

The middle knife is a 6⅝ inch typical Bowie form blade stamped "J. RUSSELL & Co/GREEN RIVER WORKS," with trademark on the ricasso, brass crossguards with beaded finials, horn scales with German silver escutcheon.

The bottom hunting knife has a 6 inch blade stamped "J. RUSSELL & Co/GREEN RIVER/WORKS" with trademark at the ricasso, German silver ferrule, checkered rosewood handle, in the original dark brown leather scabbard.

The top knife on the right is a 7¾ inch spear point blade stamped "J. RUSSELL & Co/GREEN RIVER WORKS," with trademark at the ricasso, simple brass crossguard, staghorn scales with German silver escutcheon, in an old leather scabbard.

The middle knife is a folding pocket knife with 4¼ inch blade with clipped point and sawtooth back, signed "RUSSEL" on the ricasso, "R" and Arrow trademark on both sides of the bolster, stained bone scales.

The bottom knife has "NAVY KNIFE" etched on the 3½ inch blade, the ricasso stamped "diamond R diamond"/J. RUSSELL & Co./GREEN RIVER," rosewood scales.

Richard A. Bourne Co., Inc.

From left to right, top to bottom:

8" spear point blade knife stamped "B.G.I. Co/Bridgeport, Conn/No 501," German silver oval crossguard, black hard rubber grips with stag horn pattern, in the original brown leather scabbard.

7¾" classic Bowie-form blade stamped "FAITH' at the ricasso, German silver crossguard and escutcheon, stag horn scales with old brown leather scabbard.

Three 19th century brass molds for casting bullets, the upper being a three gang mold for 18, 17 and 14 mm balls. The middle single gang mold casts a 14mm ball, while the bottom mold, missing the handles, casts two 13mm balls.

Richard A. Bourne Co., Inc.

Unmarked early saddle flanked by a vintage rifle scabbard and a venerable pair of Batwing chaps with pockets and concho decorations.

Billy the Kid Museum

Spurs belonging to Billy the Kid, showing the silver wrappings which are inlaid with the suits of cards.

Billy the Kid Museum

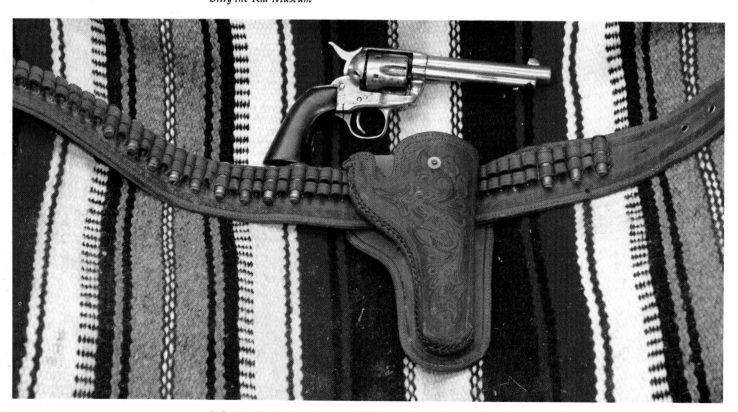

Colt Single Action Army Model revolver, but reduced to half size, serial number 280. Accompanied by original tooled leather holster and double loop cartridge belt.

Billy the Kid Museum

Winchester Model 1886 Carbine and original rifle scabbard that belonged to Billy the Kid, notorious outlaw of the West.

Billy the Kid Museum

An early pair of tapaderos with silver conchos.

Billy the Kid Museum

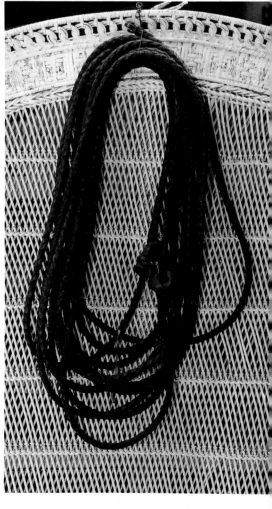

A rawhide reata used by Jesus Silva.

Billy the Kid Museum

YUMA TERRITORIAL PRISON

"On July 1, 1876, the first seven inmates entered the Territorial Prison at Yuma and were locked into the new cells they had built themselves."
A total of 3,069 prisoners, including 29 women, lived within these adobe walls during the 33 years of its operation. Their crimes ranged from murder, polygamy, and theft, with grand larceny being the most common. A majority served only portions of their sentences due to the ease with which paroles were obtained. One hundred twelve persons died in the prison, most from tuberculosis, which was common throughout the territory. Of the many prisoners who attempted to escape, 26 were successful and eight died from gunshot wounds. No executions took place at the prison because capital punishment was administered by the county governments.

"Despite an infamous reputation, written evidence indicates hat the prison was humanely administered and was a model institution for its time. The only punishments were the dark cell for inmates who broke prison regulations, and the ball and chain for those who tried to escape. Prisoners had free time when they handcrafted many items to be sold at public bazaars held at the prison on Sundays after church services. Prisoners also had regular medical attention and access to a good hospital."

Schooling was available for convicts, and many learned to read and write in prison. One of the first "public" libraries in the territory was built at the prison, and the fee charged to visitors for a tour of the institution was used to purchase books. One of the earliest electrical generating plants in the West furnished power for lights and ran a ventilator system in the cell block.

"By 1907, the prison was severely overcrowded and there was no room on Prison Hill for expansion. The convicts constructed a new facility in Florence, Arizona. The last prisoner left Yuma on Sept. 15, 1909."

The Yuma Union High School occupied the buildings from 1910 to 1914. Empty cells provided free lodging for hobos riding the freights in the 1920s, and sheltered many homeless families during the depression. Townspeople considered the complex as a source of free building materials. This, plus fires, weathering and railroad construction, destroyed the prison walls and all buildings except the cells, main gate and guard tower. These provide a glimpse of convict life a century ago."

From a brochure put out by the Arizona State Parks.

Early picture of the entrance to Yuma Territorial Prison.
Arizona State Parks

Sally Port within Yuma Territorial Prison. This is the only original adobe structure remaining at the prison.

Arizona State Parks

Main guard tower outside the walls of the Yuma Territorial Prison.

Arizona State Parks

Entrance to Yuma Territorial Prison, showing the heavy strapped outer and inner doors.

Arizona State Parks

Closer view of the main guard tower. Note the round stone water tank upon which the structure is built.

Arizona State Parks

Yuma Territorial Prison building, dated 1875. Note the heavily barred entrance and adjacent guard station.

Arizona State Parks

View of interior barred doorway in Yuma Territorial Prison. Note the period prisoner's uniform, often accompanied by a cowboy hat.

Arizona State Parks

Close up view of the heavy riveted strap iron entrance way. It was the boast of the prison authorities that no prisoner ever escaped from the Yuma Territorial Prison.

Arizona State Parks

Internal passageway within Yuma Territorial Prison. It is interesting to note the arched strap iron ceiling of the entryway beyond the entrance.

Arizona State Parks

Interior entryway at Yuma Territorial Prison.

Arizona State Parks

Close-up view of interior entryway. Note the interesting way the strap iron door is hung.

Arizona State Parks

Close up of the cell entrance, Yuma Territorial Prison.

Arizona State Parks

Interior courtyard view inside of Yuma Territorial Prison, showing entrances to cells.

Arizona State Parks

Interior view of six-man cell within the inner courtyard. These cells were open to the weather year in and year out, with many men perishing from tuberculosis as a result. In order to relieve overcrowding, some cells were dug directly into the hillsides.

Arizona State Parks

Six-man cell, Yuma Territorial Prison, showing the rudimentary accommodations for the prisoners.

Arizona State Parks

Colt Single Action .45 caliber revolver used by guards at Yuma Territorial Prison.

Arizona State Parks

Winchester Model 1876 .45-.60 caliber rifle used by guards at Yuma Territorial Prison.

Arizona State Parks

Ball and chain used as punishment for prisoners at Yuma Territorial Prison.

Arizona State Parks

Handcuffs and leg shackle used at Yuma Territorial Prison.

Arizona State Parks

Heavy leg irons used to hobble prisoners. Yuma Territorial Prison.

Arizona State Prison

Close-up side view of original wagon used to transport prisoners. Yuma Territorial Prison.

Arizona State Parks

Model of the Yuma Territorial Prison on the outskirts of Yuma, Arizona. Situated on the Bluffs overlooking the Colorado river, this prison was built after the Civil War to incarcerate criminals sentenced in the Arizona Territories.

Arizona State Parks

Silver-plated marshal's badge, dated 1886 with the serial number 15 & 556.

Dennis Bailey

Henry Alonzo "Lon" Ford, as a boy and teenager in the cow camps, he was called "The Kid," and later wrote a book by that title. For a short time he was running from the law. Later he became the sheriff of Clark County, Kansas, serving from 1932 to 1946.

Pioneer Museum, Ashland, Kansas

WYATT EARP'S OUTHOUSE HANDLE

Even the rugged Wyatt Earp was required to answer the call of nature. Exhibited here for your utter amazement is his original outhouse handle still attached to a portion of his private facility. Perhaps this was his only refuge from the rough and tumble days of early Tombstone.

Souvenirs of the Old Frontier! Wyatt Earp's outhouse handle.

Arizona State Parks

Buffalo Bill, Chief of Scouts and Guide for U.S. Army Poster. A younger Cody radiates from a strong central image of him resting, almost on his laurels. At the top, he is a wagon master for the firm of Russell, Major and Co., hauling freight at the age of 12, in 1858. He is a Pony Express rider in 1861, traveling 18 miles an hour, and on the other side of the Congressional Medal of Honor bestowed on him, he is trapping beavers. He is a stage driver of overland mail in 1862, and, as a justice of the peace, he married a couple at Fort McPherson, Nebraska. In the middle left, he is scouting, and to the right, he is being chased by Indians. He is shown killing Cheyenne chief Yellowhand in 1876 and, opposite this, killing 69 buffalo in one run without saddle.

The major scene at the bottom shows "General Sheridan appointing Buffalo Bill guide for the Grand Duke Alexis and Royal Cortege on their great American buffalo hunt, 1872. Among the trophies is a buffalo head with diamond eyes presented to him by Sir John Watts Garland, whom he had guided in a hunting party in the winter of 1870-71, and a diamond pin and medal presented by the Duke Alexis.

Circa 1888, measuring 20" by 25".

Witherell's Americana Auctions

Colt Lightning .44 caliber Slide Action rifle, marked on the tang, "S.F.P.D. 83." One of 300 such rifles issued to the San Francisco Police Department in the 1890s.

Witherell's Americana Auctions

Full view of the Deluxe Winchester Model 1886, .38-.56 caliber rifle owned by Buffalo Bill.

Witherell's Americana Auctions

Closeup of Buffalo Bill's Winchester Deluxe Model 1886, 38-56 caliber lever action rifle, serial number 38782, with 26" octagonal barrel. Notice the excellent case hardening on the receiver, as well as the checkering on the pistol grip and forestock.

Below the rifle is the Model 1860 U.S. Staff and Field Officer's engraved sword presented by Buffalo Bill Cody. The inscription reads: "Presented to Major A. Gerald Hull of Saratoga Citizens Corp Staff. By Hon. W.F. Cody— "Buffalo Bill," Feb. 28, 86." Manufactured by Raymond and Whitlock, New York. Gold-etched blade, with bronze mounted nickel scabbard.

Witherell's Americana Auctions

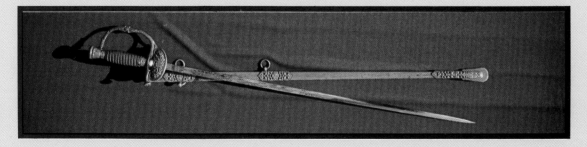

Full view of the Cody presentation sword and scabbard.

Witherell's Americana Auctions

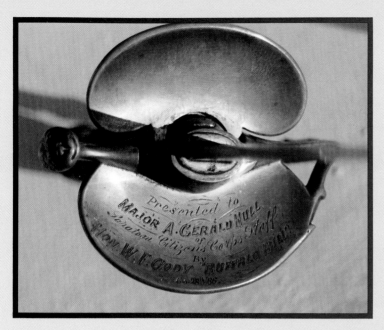

Closeup of the engraving on the clam shell guard of the presentation sword.

Witherell's Americana Auctions

Dr. Albert Wigglesworth with his younger brother, Jack, and his favorite burro "Jinny." Waterfall ranch, Animas Valley near Durango, Colorado, 1875.

Jack Wigglesworth

Waterfall Ranch, Animas Valley, near Durango, Colorado. Homestead of Thomas H. Wigglesworth, railroad surveyor, and the home of Dr. Albert Wigglesworth while he was growing up.

Jack Wigglesworth

Ignacio, Chief of the Southern Utes, and a friend of Dr. Wigglesworth. Taken near Durango, Colorado in 1901.

Jack Wigglesworth

Home of Dr. and Mrs. Wigglesworth after their wedding on December 24, 1901. Fort Lewis, Colorado.

Jack Wigglesworth

Refer in reply to the following :

EDUCATION.

55440-1900

INCLOSURE.

Department of the Interior,

OFFICE OF INDIAN AFFAIRS,

Washington, D. C., Nov. 12, 1900.

Albert M. Wigglesworth,

Cortez, Colo.

Sir:

You are hereby appointed, under the conditions printed hereon, to the position of Physician in the Ft. Lewis School, Colo.,

at a salary of $1000 per annum.

Your salary will begin when you take the oath of office and enter upon duty. The oath of office may be taken before a notary public, or other officer qualified to administer oaths, and should be forwarded at once to this office A blank form of oath is herewith inclosed.

As this appointment is by virtue of the Civil Service law, the same is probationary until June 30, 1901.

You will be obliged to pay your traveling expenses to the school, and your board while there; but quarters will be provided you at the school under conditions prescribed in Indian School Rule 123. Board in school employees' mess will cost about $ 14 *per month, for each person.*

Please telegraph me at once whether or not you accept this appointment. If you accept report for duty at once to Dr. Thomas H. Breen, Superintendent Ft. Lewis Indian School, Hesperus, Colo. Railroad station, Hesperus, on Rio Grande Southern Rwy., via Denver and Durango; school 4 miles from depot; private team.

Very respectfully,

_____

Acting *Commissioner*

W.A.M.
13977b1m3-1900

RCB

[SEE OTHER SIDE.]

A copy of the formal contract between Dr. Albert Wigglesworth and the Bureau of the Interior, Office of Indian Affairs for his term of service as physician at the Fort Lewis School, Colorado for the princely sum of $1,000 annually.

Jack Wigglesworth

Cowboy movie posters, one of the latest interests in cowboy collecting.

The Jordan Gallery

An early Roy Rogers movie poster for "Mackintosh and T.J."

The Jordan Gallery

Vera Ralston and Joan Leslie were the female leads in "Jubilee Trail," also starring Forrest Tucker and John Russell.

The Jordan Gallery

James Stewart, Dean Martin, Raquel Welch and George Kennedy star in "Bandolero."

The Jordan Gallery

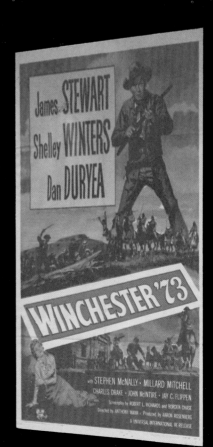

Advertisement for the famous movie "Winchester '73," starring Jimmy Stewart.

The Jordan Gallery

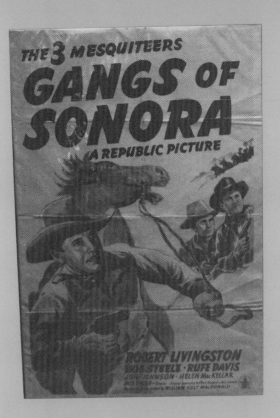

The Three Mesquiteers, in "Gangs of Sonora," starred Robert Livingston, Bob Steele and Rufe Davis.

The Jordan Gallery

Undoubtedly one of the most famous western movies to come out of Hollywood, "Shane," starring Alan Ladd, was also one of the best westerns made.

The Jordan Gallery

"Strange Gamble," starred William Boyd, or, as he was better known, "Hopalong Cassidy."

The Jordan Gallery

Henry Fonda, in one of his many western roles, starred in "Welcome to Hard Times."

The Jordan Gallery

Joel McCrea did an excellent job in depicting the life of
William Cody in "Buffalo Bill."

The Jordan Gallery

With a host of stars, MGM produced "How The West
Was Won."

The Jordan Gallery

Poster for "Young Fury," with Rory Calhoun, Virginia
Mayo, Lon Chaney and William Bendix.

The Jordan Gallery

One of the earliest heros of the western movie, Tom Mix, a real-life cowboy, starred in "Daredevil's Reward."

The Jordan Gallery

"Custer's Last Stand," as produced for Anheuser-Busch Brewing Co., a saloon standard!

The Jordan Gallery

"Days of 49" canvas whiskey sign. This icon of the West depicts the westward movement to the California gold fields. What more could you ask for? Cowboys, Indians, wagon trains, guns and whiskey. Meyerfeld, Mitchell and Co., San Francisco, Lithographer, H.S. Crocker Co., S.F., circa 1900. Measures 24" by 36".

Witherell's Americana Auctions

Broadside poster of Dodson's Worlds Fair Shows, depicting a violent attack by Indians on settlers staunchly defending themselves.

The Jordan Gallery

Movie Poster of "The Life of Buffalo Bill in Three Reels." The scene at the top shows a battle with Indians and the caption reads, "First scalp for Custer." Below sits Cody on a white horse. Measures 42" by 28".

Witherell's Americana Auctions

Price Guide

Values vary immensely according to the condition of the piece, the location of the market, and the overall quality of the design and manufacture. Condition is always of paramount importance in assigning a value. Prices vary by geographic location and those at specialty antique shows will vary from those at general shows. And, of course, being in the right place at the right time may make all the difference.

All these factors make it impossible to create an absolutely accurate reference, but we can offer a guide.

To use this guide it is necessary to know that the left hand number is the **page** number.

The letters following it indicate the **position** of the photograph on the page: T=top, L=left, TL=top left, TC=top center, TR=top right, C=center, CL=center left, CR=center right, R=right, B=bottom, BL=bottom left, BC=bottom center, BR=bottom right.

The last letter represents the estimated **value** ranges in U.S. dollars. They coordinate to the photographs on the page, and **when more than one item appears in a photograph, the prices follow the order of the caption**. The code is as follows:

A= Up to $100
B= $100-250
C= $250-500
D= $500-1000
E= $750-1000
F= $1000-2500
G= $2500-5000
H= $5000-7500
I= $7500-10000
J= Above $10000

Page	Pos.	Value
6		J
22	L	C
	R	C
23	L	D
	R	C
24	L	C
	R	C
25	TL	C
	TR	B
	BR	A
26	T	B
	B	F
27	T	C
	B	J
28	L	D
	R	J
29	L	J
30	T	H
	B	E
31	L	E
	R	Rare
32	L	C
	R	E
33	L	D
	R	D
34	TL	D
	TR	C
	B	D
35	TR	E
	B	E
36	T	I
	CL	D
	B	D
37	TR	D

Page	Pos.	Value
	BL	A
38	TL	B
	TR	C
	B	C
39		D
40		F
41	TL	C
	B	D
42	T	F
43	T	E
	B	D
44	T	A
	CL	E
45	L	I
	C	J
46	L	J
	TR	F
	BR	F
47	TL	I
	TR	E
	BL	J
48	L	I
	R	G
49	L	D
	R	H
50	TL	H
	TR	I
	B	D
51	L	F
	R	E
52	TL	C
	TR	G
	BL	G
53	TL	J

Page	Pos.	Value
	TR	J
	BL	F
54	L	D
	TR	D
	BR	F
55	T	G
	B	H
56	T	F
	B	G
57	T	A
	B	J
58	T (all)	G
	BL	G
	BR	I
59		J
64	T	H, G, F, G
65	T	J
66		E, E, E, F, F
67	TL	J
68	T	F
	C	E
	B	D
69	T	H
	B	G
70	T	D
	C	D
	B	E
71	T	C
	C	C
	B	B
72	T	C
		C

Page	Pos.	Value
	B	C
73	T	C
	C	B
	B	C
74	T	C
	C	C
	B	D,B
75	T	F
	C	J
76	T	G
	B	J
77		G
78	T	J
	B	J
79	T	G
	Remington, F	
	Colt, E	
	Pacific Express, G	
	S&W Volcanic, F	
	S&W .38, F	
	Cooper Navy, F	
	B	I
80	T	F
	B	I
81	T	H
	B	H
82	T	H
	C	B
	B	C
83	T	C
	B	C
84	T (all)	B
85	T	B,A,B, B,A,A

Page	Pos.	Value
	B	B,B,B, A,A,A
86	TL (all)	A
	TR (all)	A
	BR	B,B,A, A,A
87	T	B
	B	B,E,C
88	TL	D,C,F
	TR (all)	D
	BL	D,D,F
89	All	C
90	T (all)	B
	B	B,B, A,A,A
101	T	I
	C	F
	B	J
102	T	J,J
	B	J
106	L	B
	R	B
107	All	B
108	All	B
109	All	B
110	T	B
	B	C
111	T	F
	CR	C
	BL	E